LYNN LENNON, who lives in Dallas, Texas, is the author of *Categorically Speaking,* a book of photographs of cats. As a free-lance photographer, she has had many interesting commissions, including one that took her to Kenya to photograph the sculptor Robert Glen and then to England to document the making of an immense equestrian sculpture by him that is to be installed in Irving, Texas. Animal images are by no means Lynn Lennon's principal interest. She has done a photo essay on the Texas artist David McManaway for his show at the Dallas Museum of Fine Arts, as well as a photodocumentary on the Louisiana sugarcane industry that is in the permanent collection of the Riverside Museum in Baton Rouge, a series on the American cowboy that has been exhibited in London, Brussels, and Paris, and a study of the residents of the Big Thicket area of Texas. There have been one-woman shows of her work in Houston, Dallas, New York, Los Angeles, Dublin, London, and other cities. Her photographs have also been exhibited in various group shows and have appeared in books, newspapers, and magazines in the United States and in Europe. Ms. Lennon was born in Dallas and studied art and English at Baylor University in Waco. Before becoming a professional photographer, she was an artist, doing paintings, silkscreen works, and assemblages.

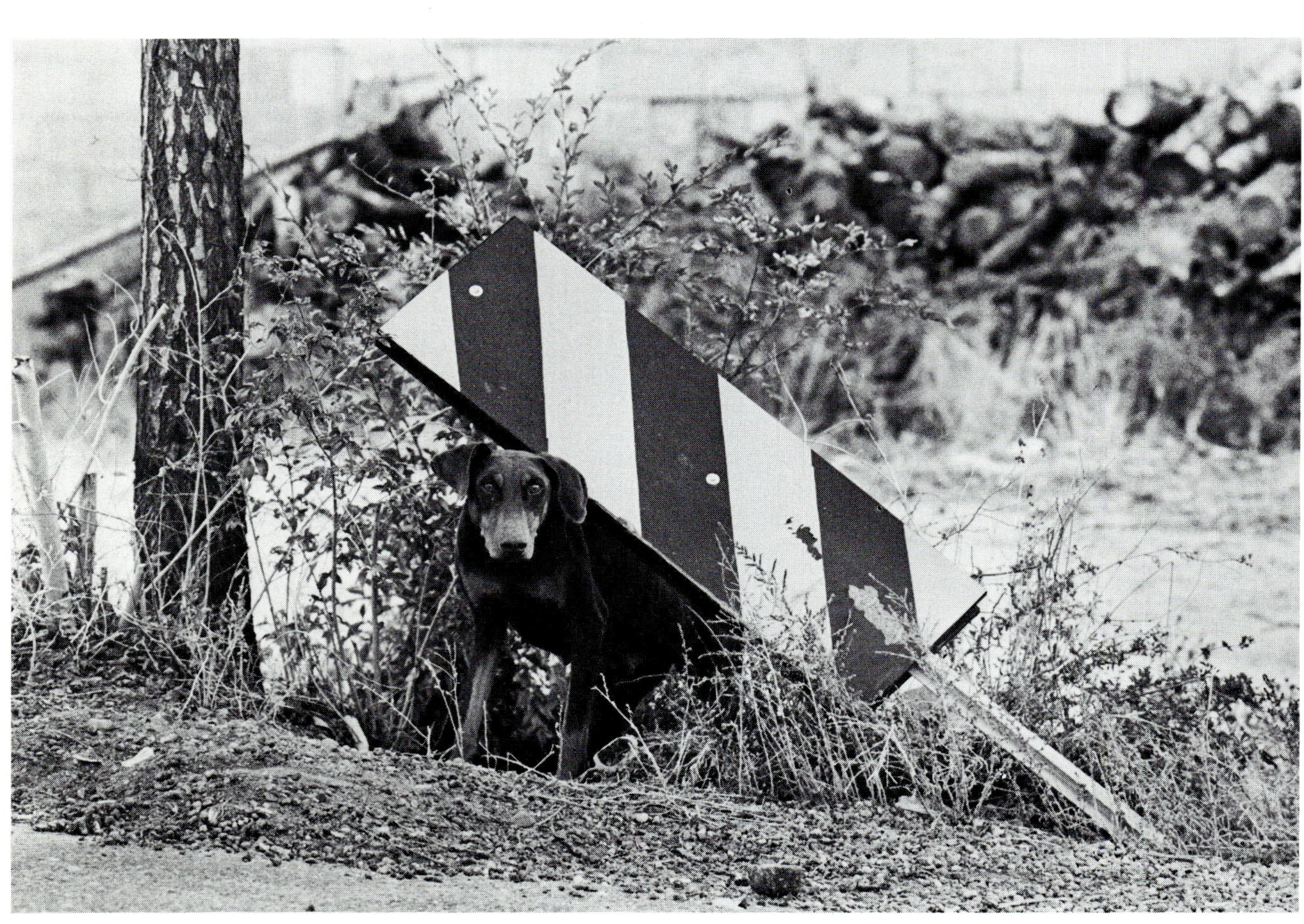

DOGMATICALLY SPEAKING

Lynn Lennon

A Studio Book THE VIKING PRESS New York

Also by Lynn Lennon
CATEGORICALLY SPEAKING

DOGMATICALLY SPEAKING

Published in 1983 by The Viking Press
A Studio Book
40 West 23rd Street
New York, N.Y. 10010

Published simultaneously in Canada by
Penguin Books Canada Limited

Library of Congress Cataloging in Publication Data
Lennon, Lynn.
Dogmatically speaking.
(A Studio book)
1. Dogs—Pictorial works. I. Title.
SF430.L46 1983 636.7'00222 82-50270
ISBN 0-670-27665-0

Printed in the United States of America
Set in Fairfield

Dogmatically Speaking

As I was photographing dogs for this book, I had a real sense of *déjà vu.* I asked for my first camera the Christmas that I was eight. For more than a year, except for taking a picture of my teddy bear and one of a horse, I photographed nothing but dogs. I carried my little black plastic Brownie Hawkeye with me everywhere and photographed every dog I saw. In some of the pictures the dogs were only a speck in the distance or were blurred, but nothing else interested me as subject matter. With this recent series of dog photographs, it seems my life has come full circle.

As this tale might indicate, I have always been a "dog person" and almost always a photographer. As very young children, my sister and I spent a lot of time making scrapbooks. My sister made scrapbooks of movie stars and I made scrapbooks of dogs. In these I pasted every picture of a dog that I found, including the small flea-powder ad that ran in many magazines with a tiny black-and-white sketch of a dog scratching and the bold, black headline: DOG NEARLY ITCHES TO DEATH.

I also remember one long hot summer day around my tenth birthday when my sister and I walked to the dime store and bought some magical incense. The instructions on a small enclosure read, "Go alone to a quiet spot. Light the incense. Write one hundred times your fondest desire and it will come true." This is a very clear memory. I am sitting barefoot at a small desk writing over and over, "I want to be a veterinarian."

I have owned nine dogs in my lifetime. Four were special. The first was Midget, a fox terrier. I was seven when I finally saved enough nickels and dimes to make the ten dollars that she cost. For as long as she lived she was the most important thing in my life. I was devastated when she was killed by an automobile. Rusty was a small short-haired mongrel that I rescued from the grade-school custodian. Scamper was a honey-colored mixed breed of great character who deserved a longer life than he had. The most recent one was Hank the beagle, a faithful friend for fourteen years.

Except for the dogs that I have personally owned, I had not had a great deal of experience with different breeds. While making these photographs I was impressed with the intelligence of the Labradors, the gentle sweetness of the Irish setters and the golden retrievers, and the playful bounciness of the Airedales and the English sheep dogs. But of all the dogs I encountered, one especially remains in my mind. He was a little mixed-breed, half-grown puppy that I saw in the lobby of a New York apartment building. I spoke to his owner, an older woman who had acquired the dog only the day before. I sat on the floor to photograph the dog from behind as he sat under her folding chair. He came to the end of his leash, climbed into my lap, and pressed himself hard against my chest. He sat this way for a long time and I didn't move. Finally his owner got up to go. As she walked down the hall to the elevator, he continued to strain at the end of his leash to get back to me. The memory of his warm little body pressed close to mine stays with me.

It was in that same apartment building that I gave another woman quite a start. A friend of mine lived in the building and was taking me to various apartments where she said I would find interesting dogs. The bell rang, and when the door was opened my friend introduced me. She said I had come to shoot the dog and that we had already discussed it with her daughter, who had given her permission. The woman gasped and put her hand to her breast. "Oh," she said, "why are you going to do that? Did he bite someone?" We explained that we meant to shoot photographs, but she was so unnerved that we excused ourselves and moved on.

I was amazed to see the plush life enjoyed by some of these dogs: the Saint Bernard riding in the Rolls-Royce in solitary splendor, and the Pekingese that sleeps in the antique French doll's bed and owns an extensive custom-made wardrobe. The Labrador seen floating on his raft also has his own inflatable boat, powered by a small outboard motor, in which he putters around the pool. But the dogs that got to me were the ones like the little lost dog on the street in Oaxaca dragging her chain along the sidewalk, the black-and-white puppy who gazed pensively from his place at the top of the steps, the blind man's dog waiting patiently at his feet all day, and the stray on the street corner asleep with his paw over his nose. These little ones with their air of vulnerability really touched my heart.

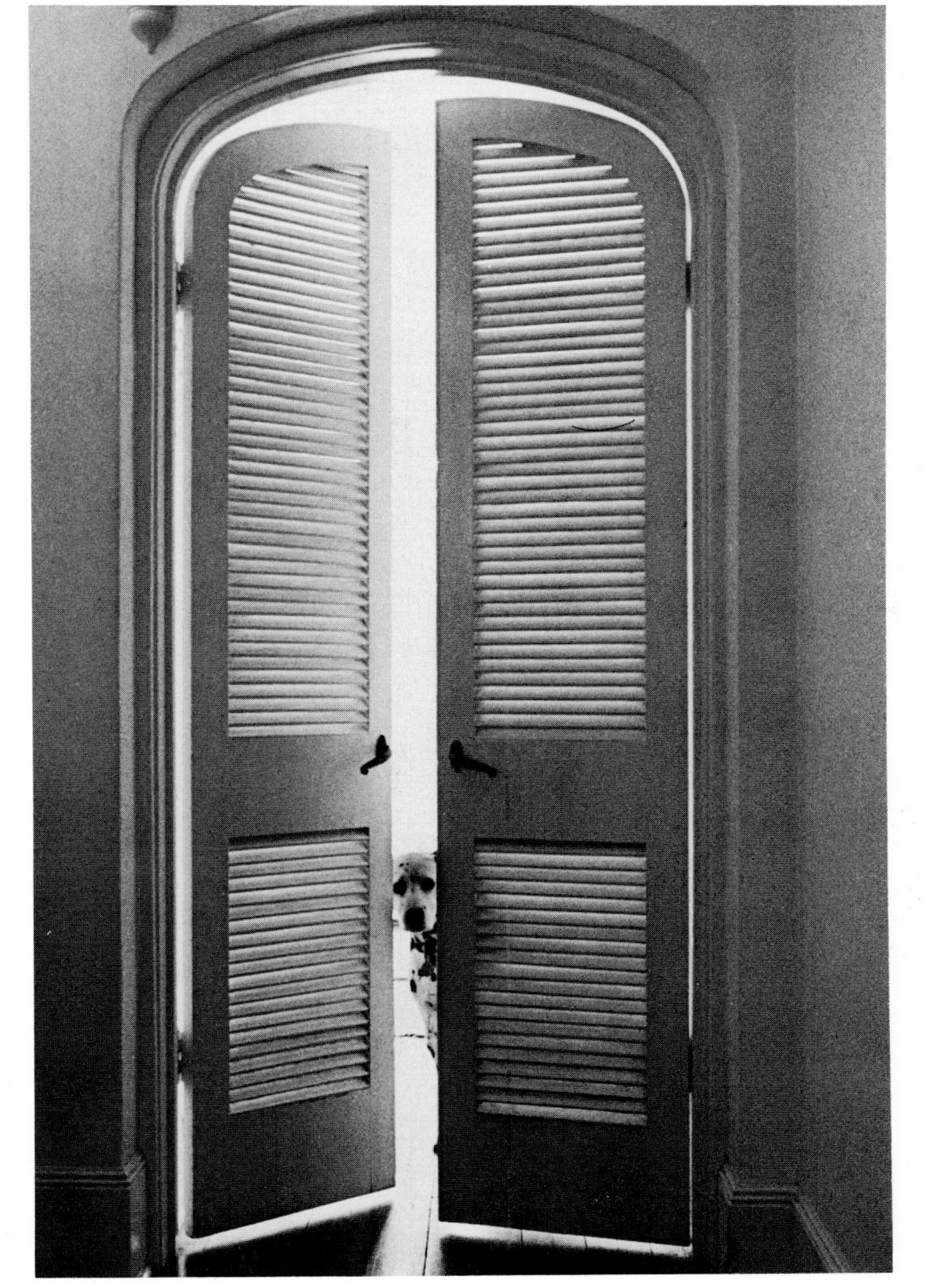

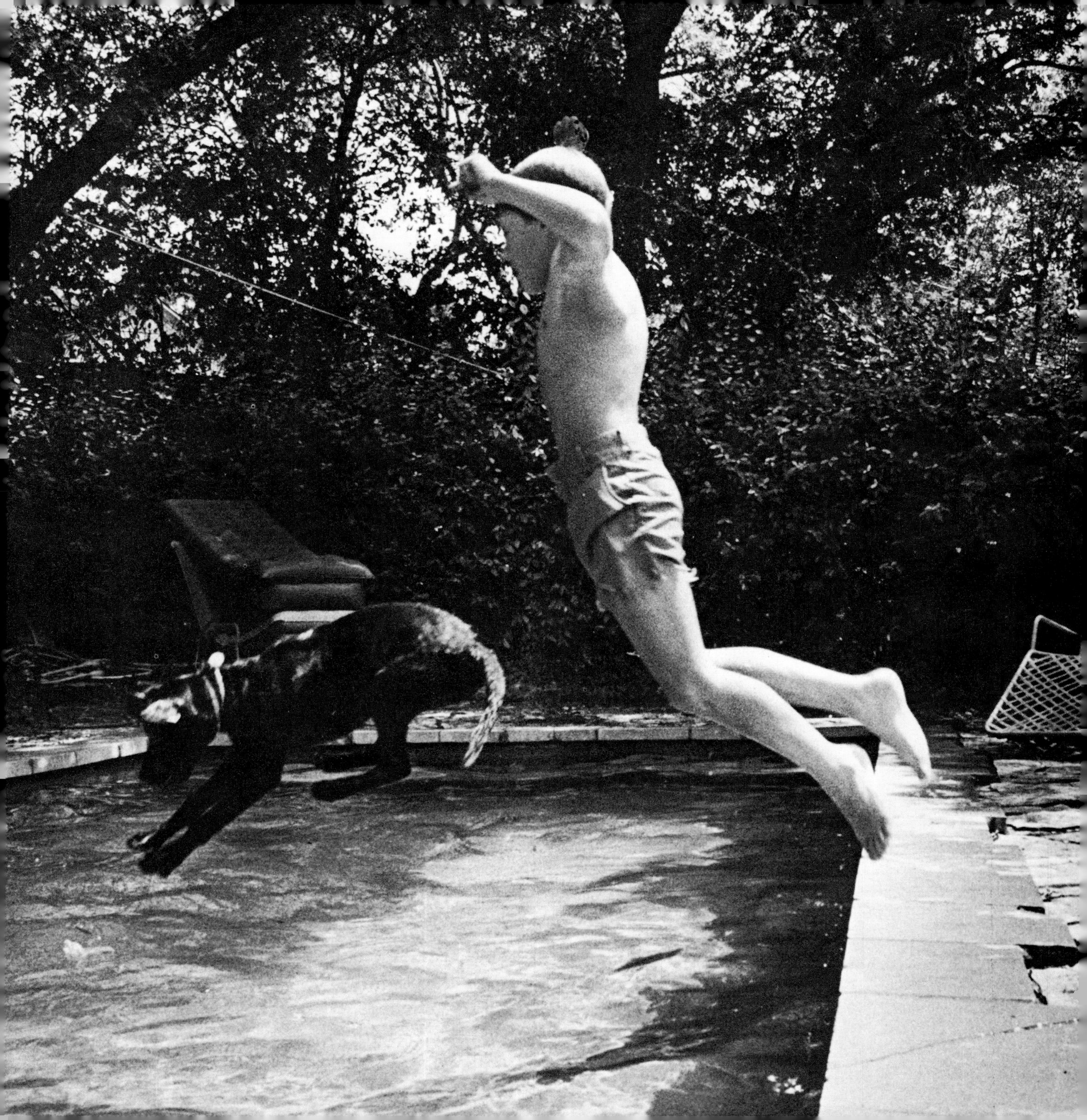

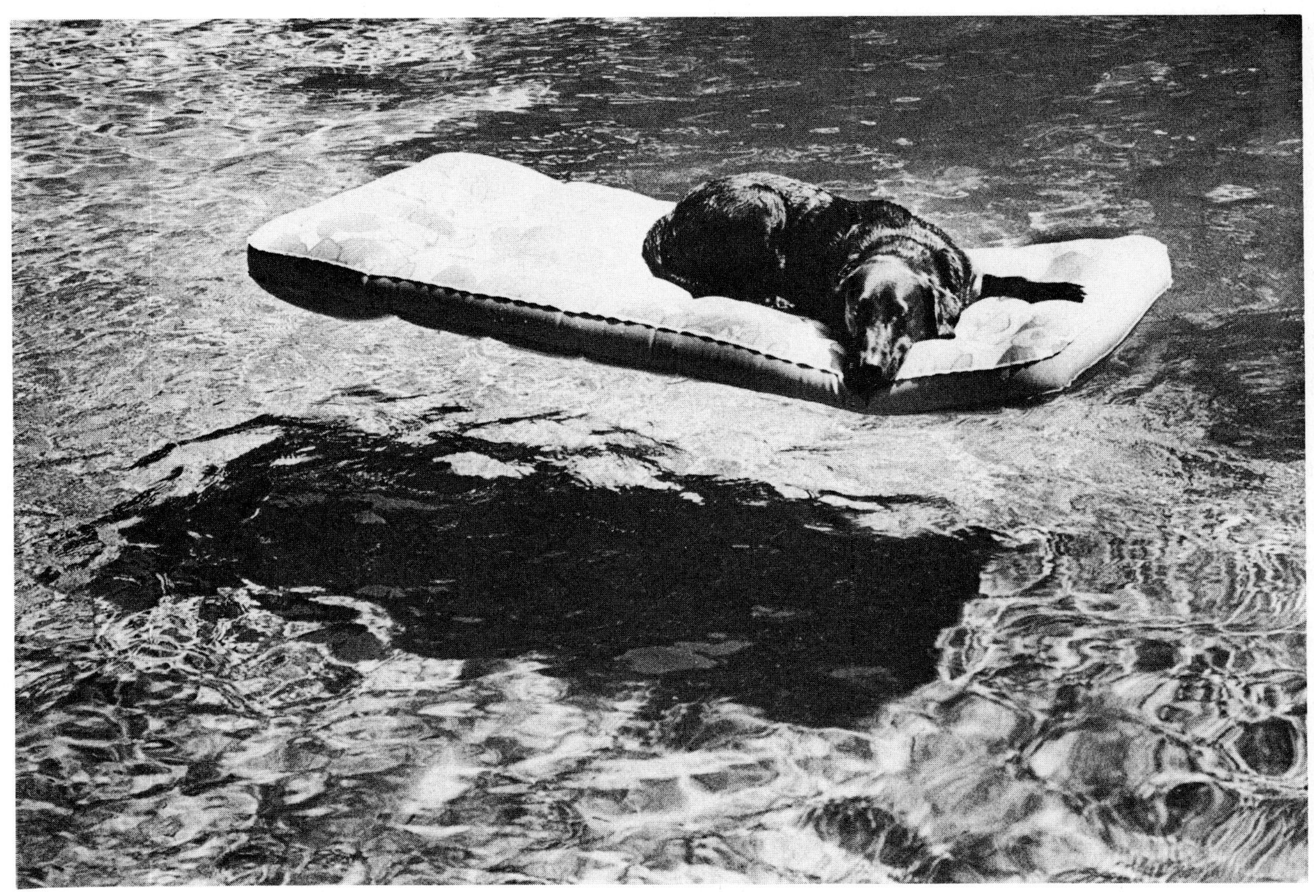

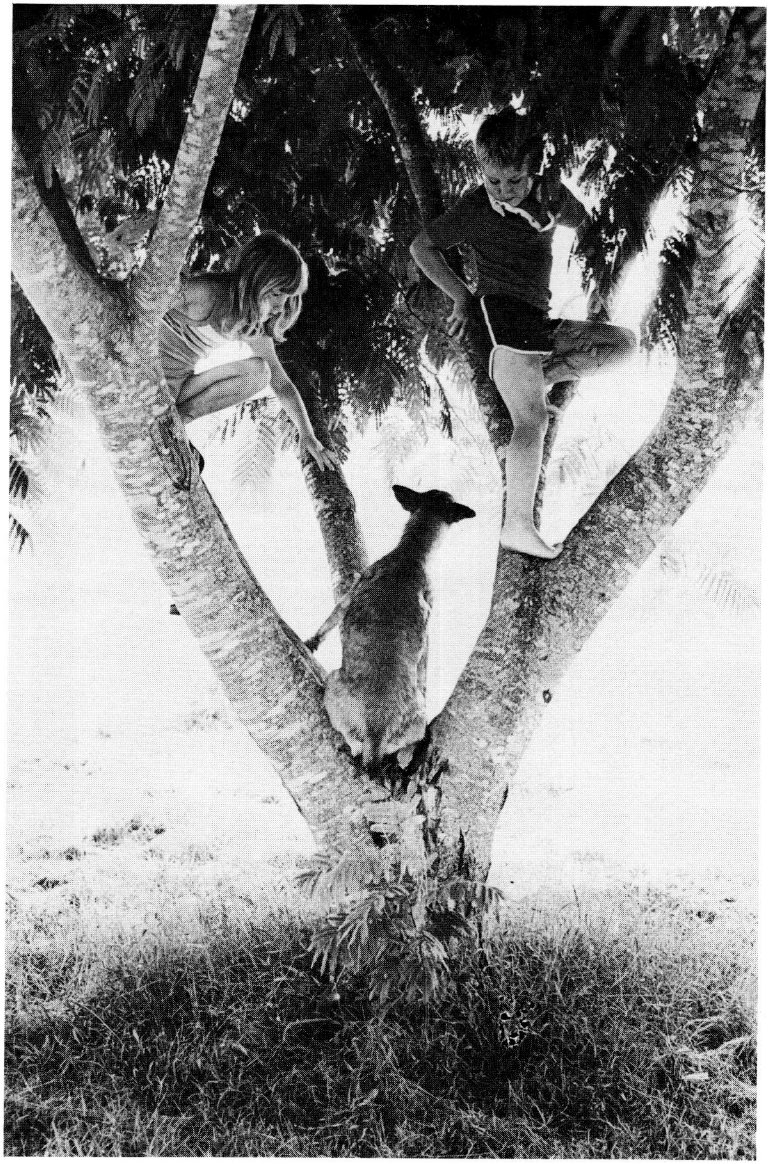

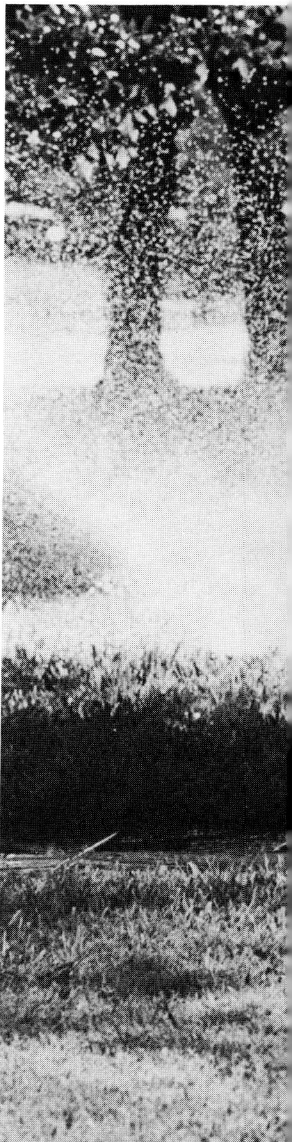

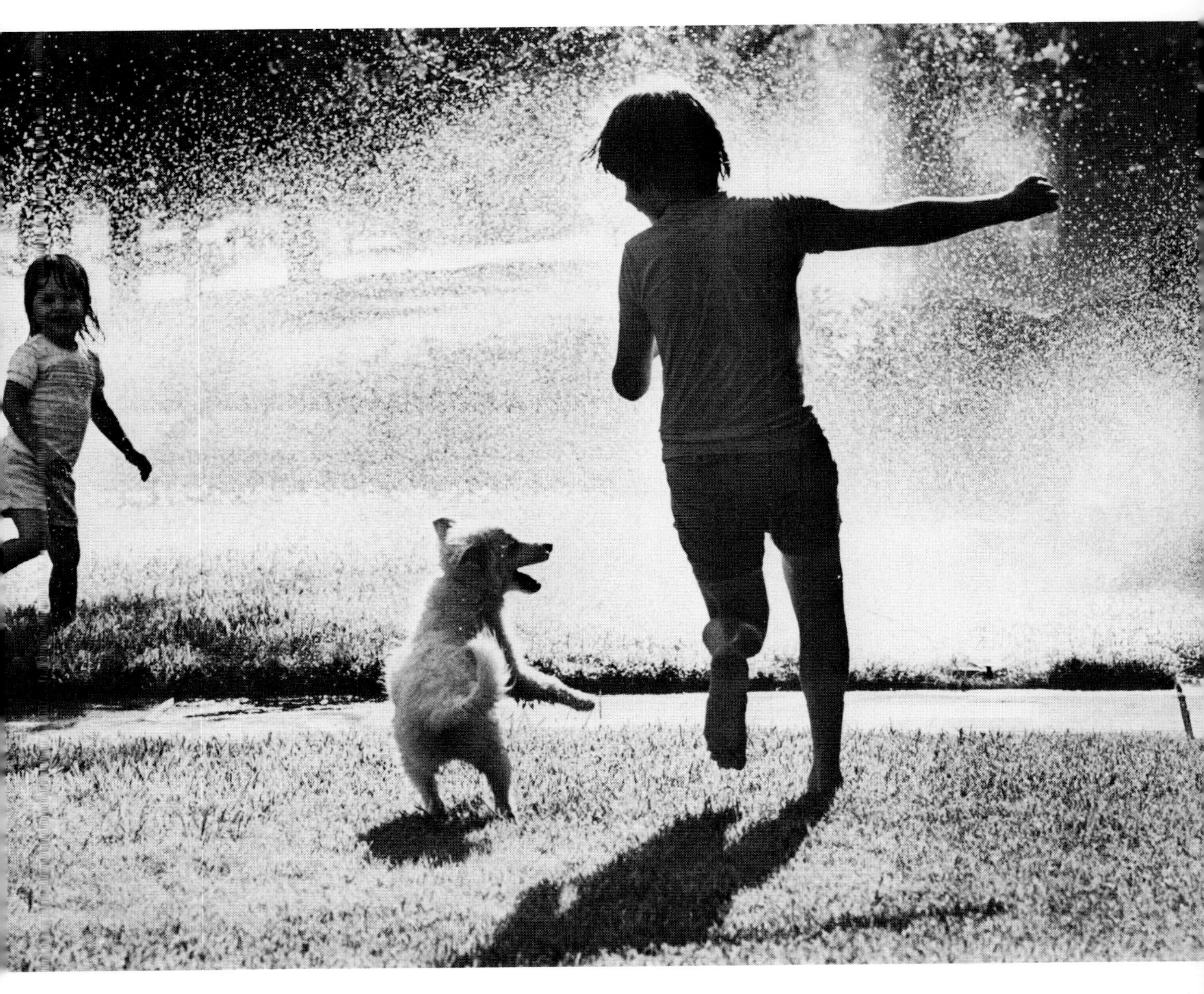

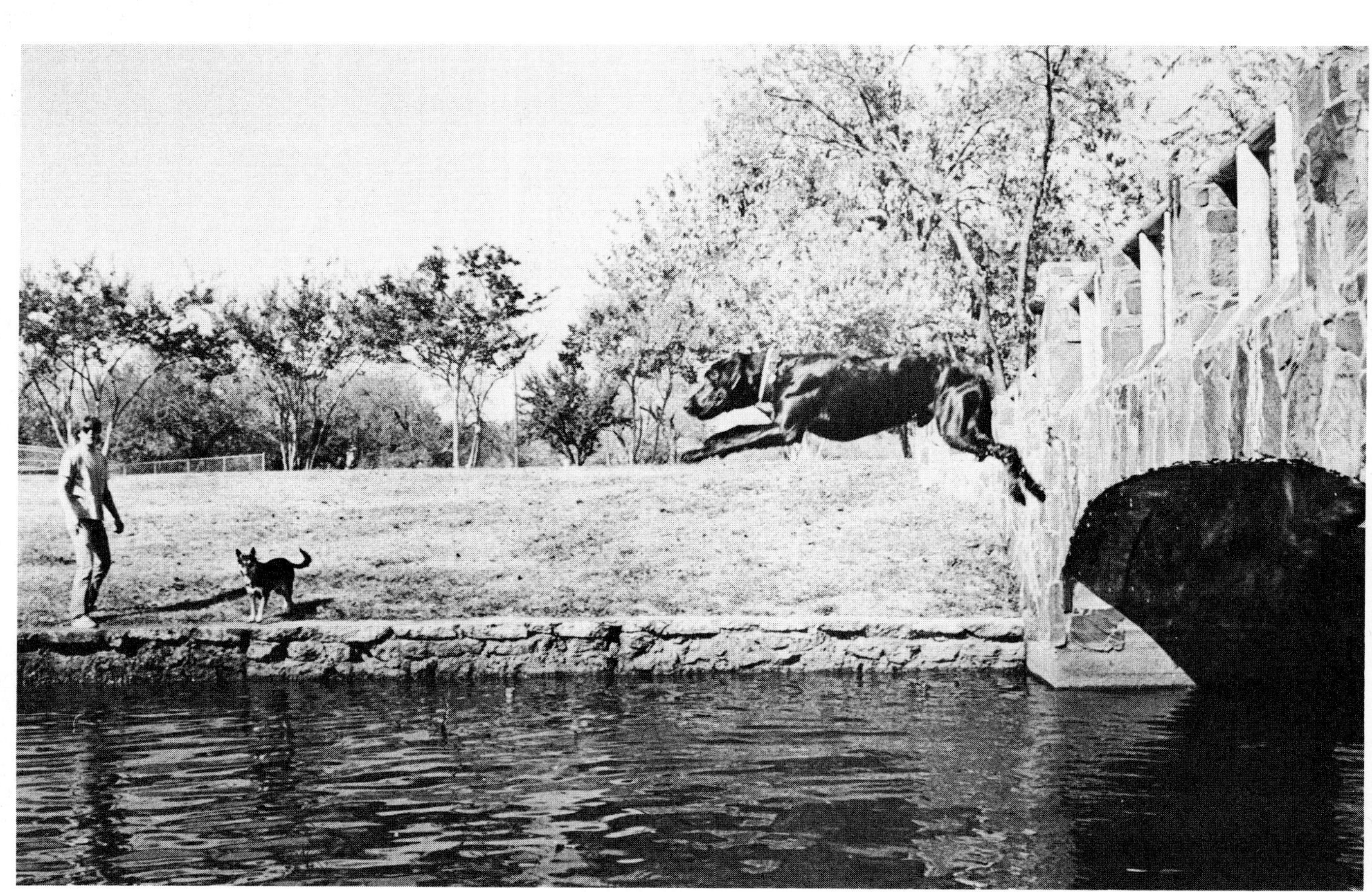

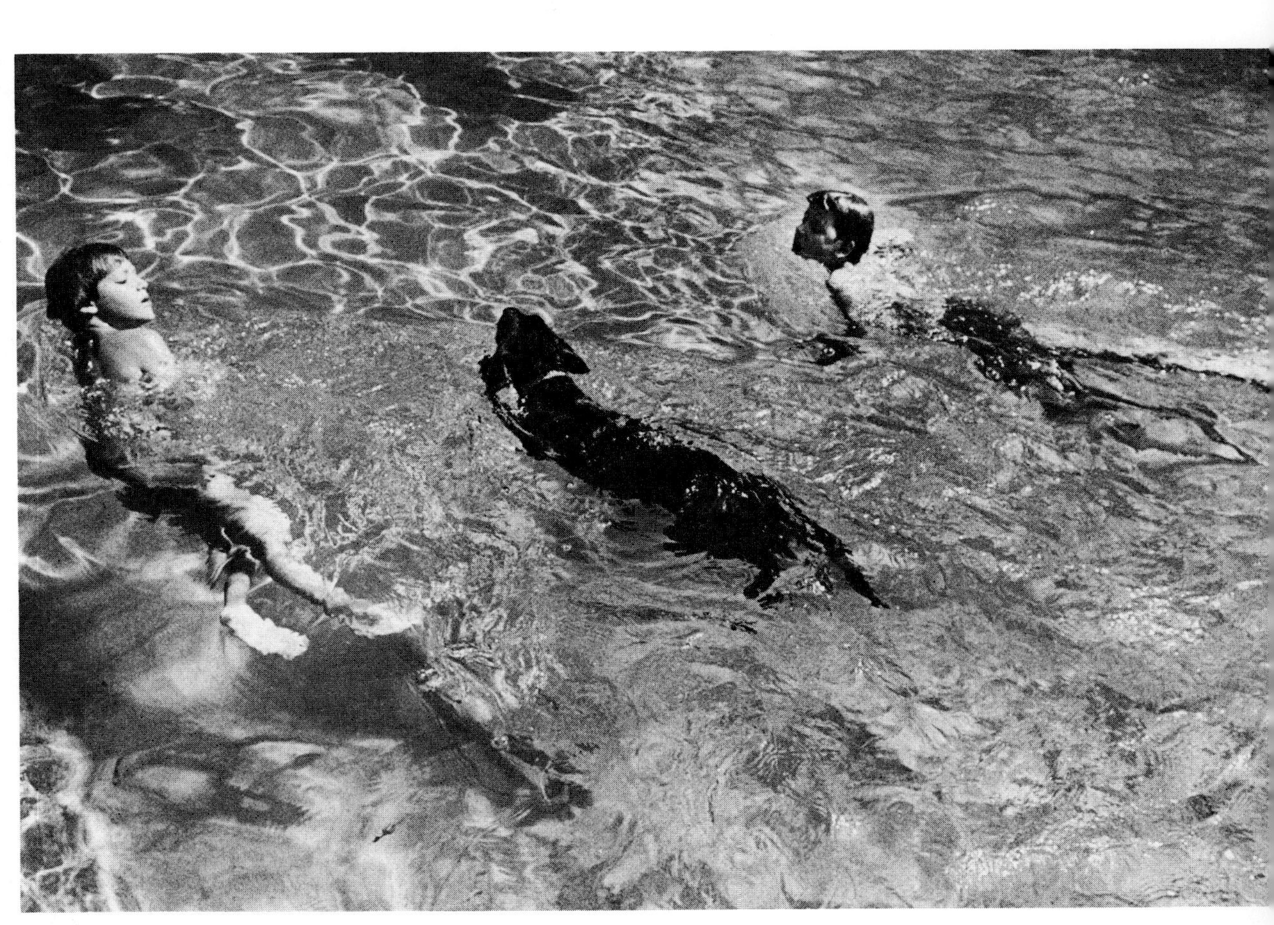

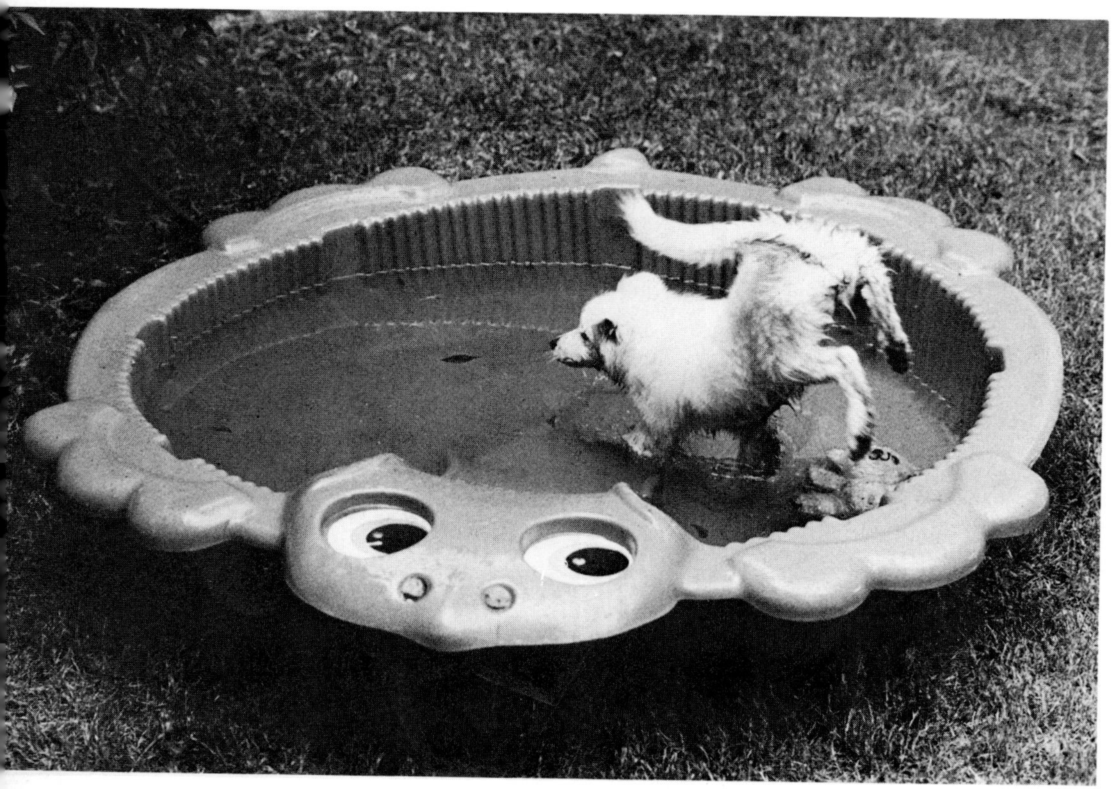

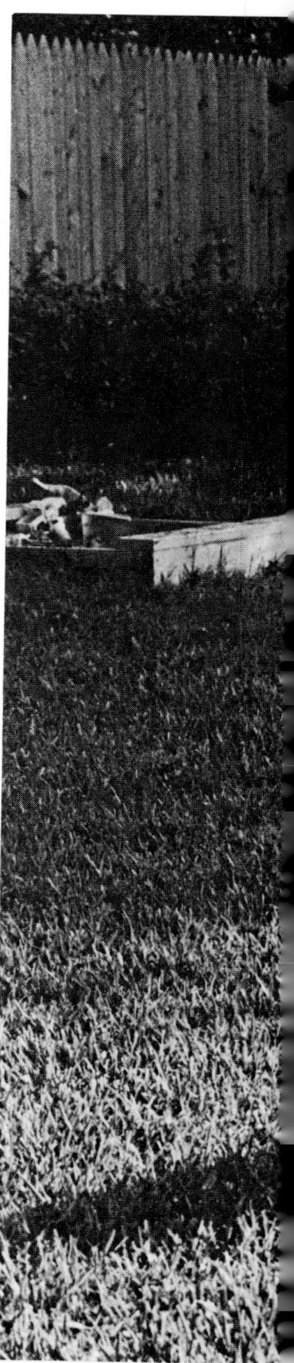

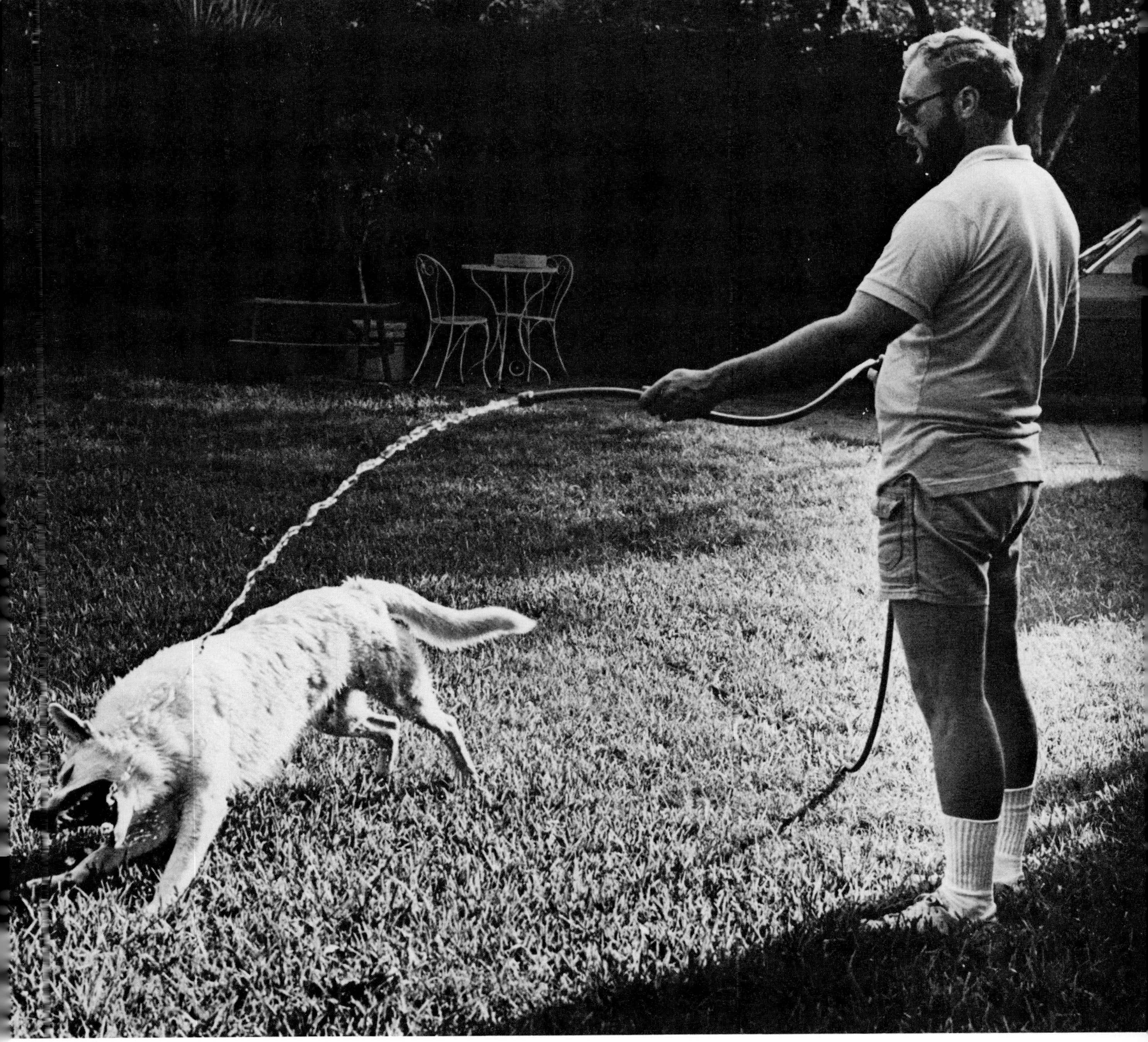

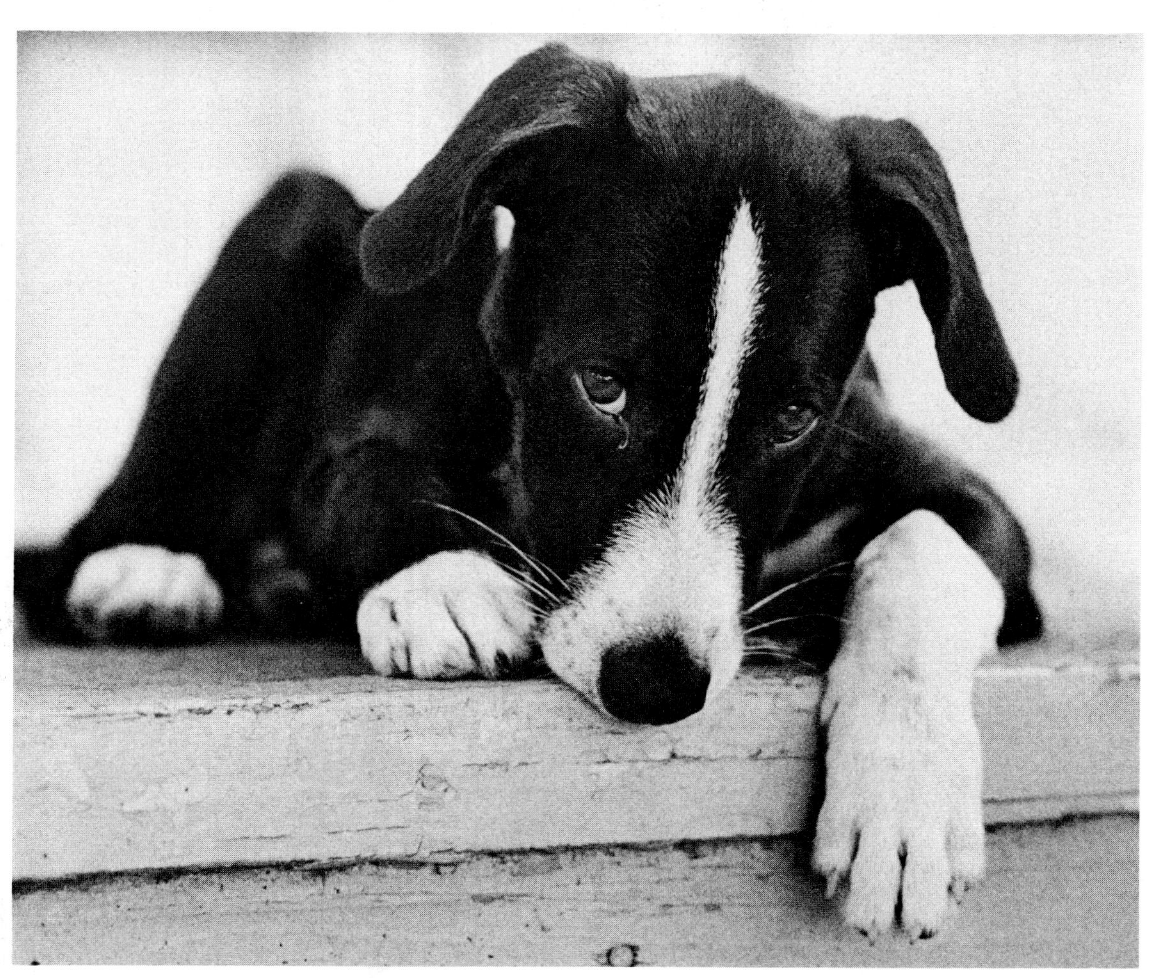

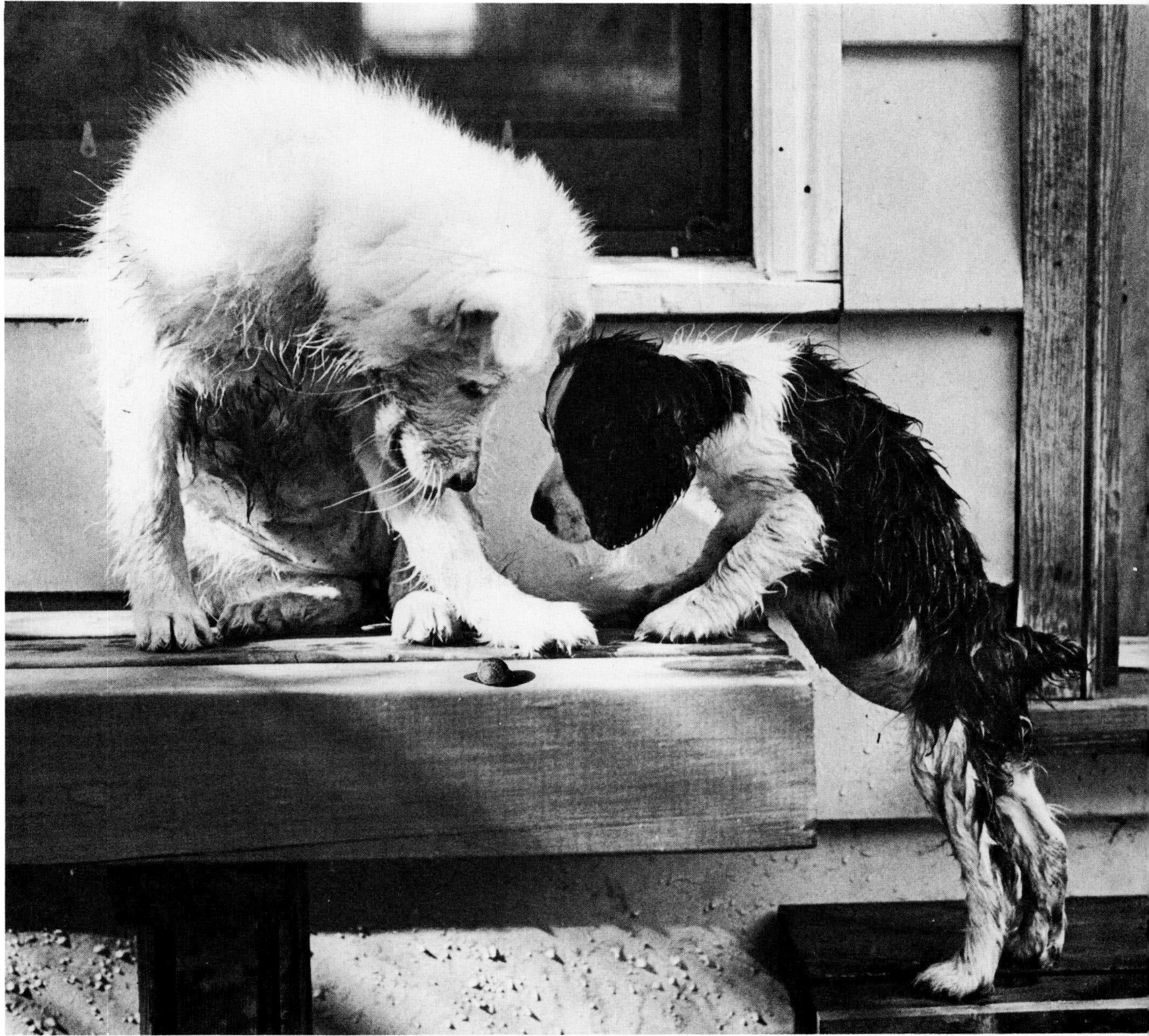

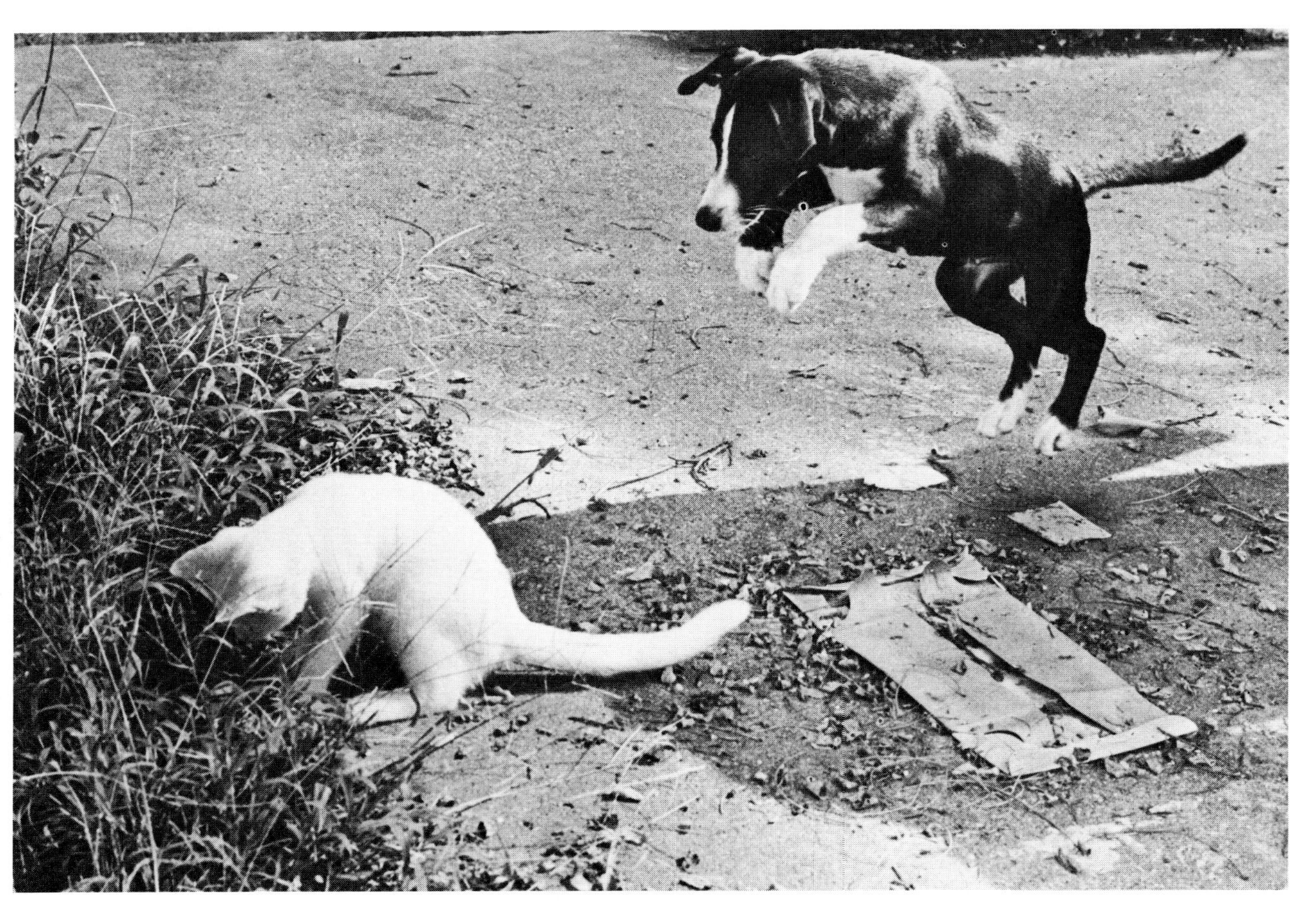

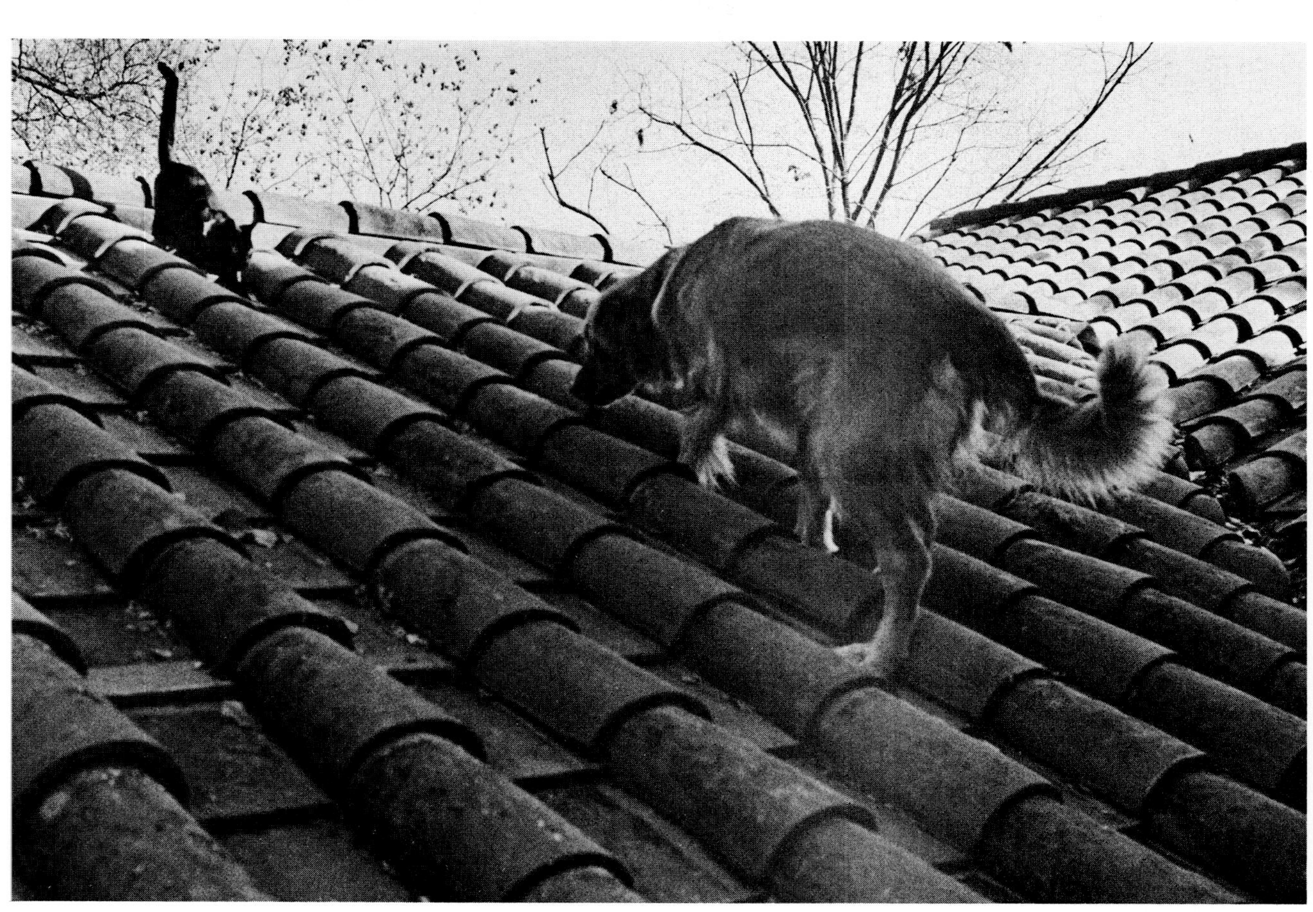

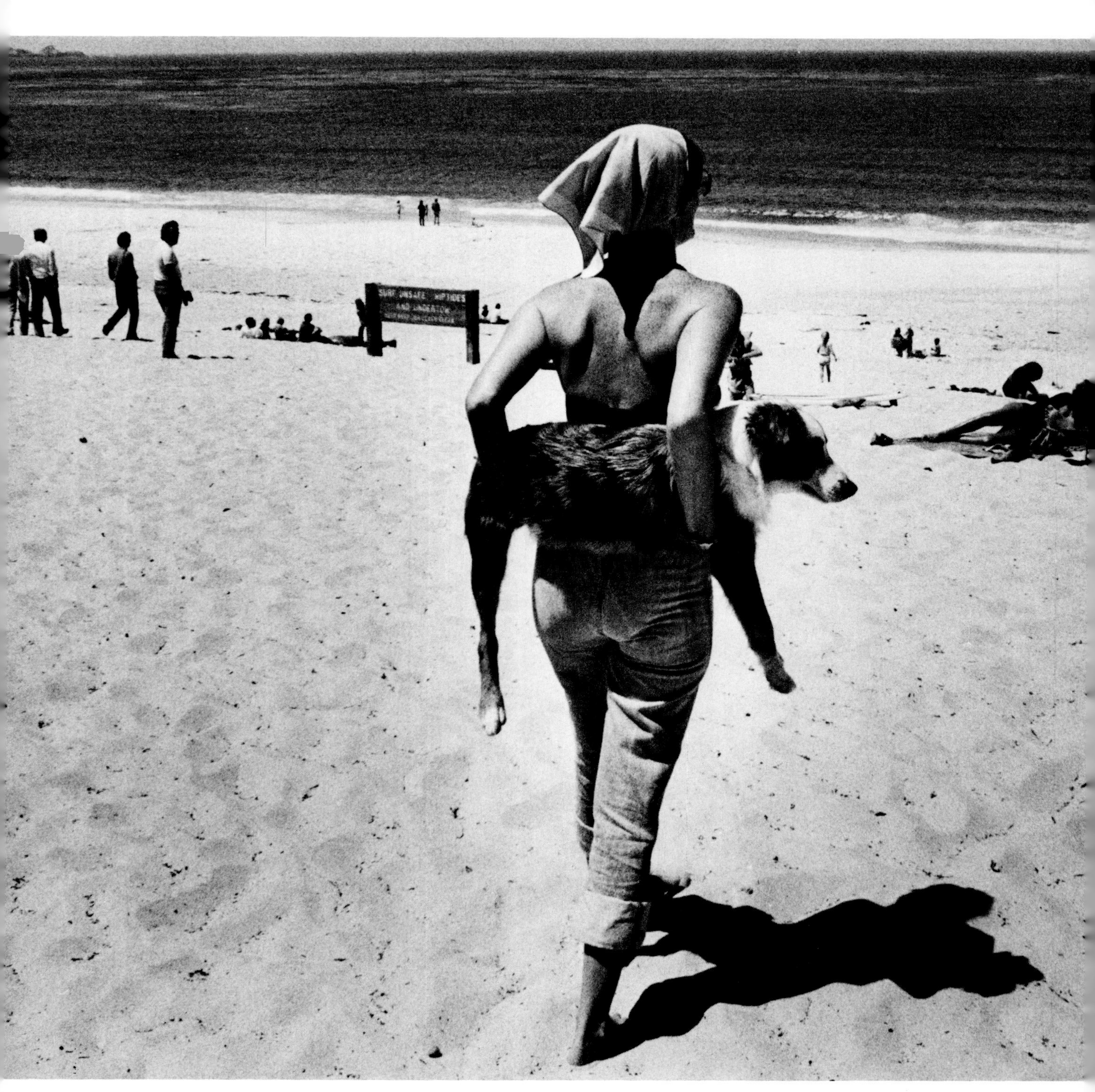

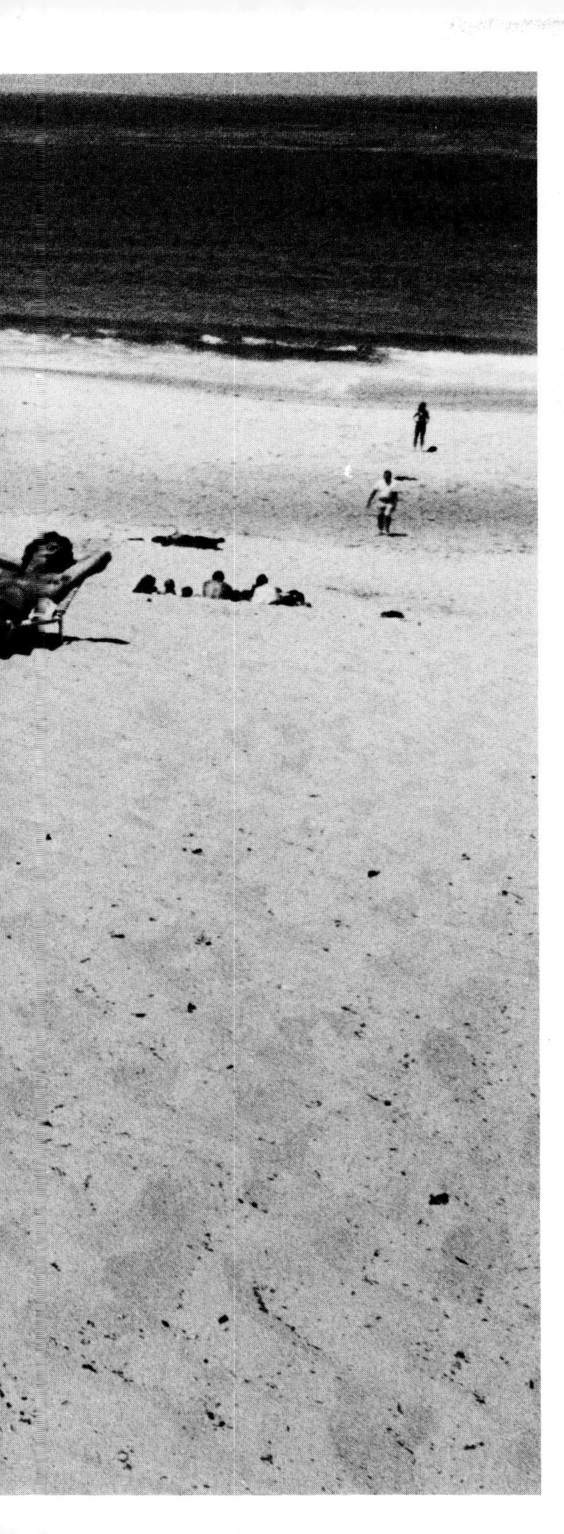

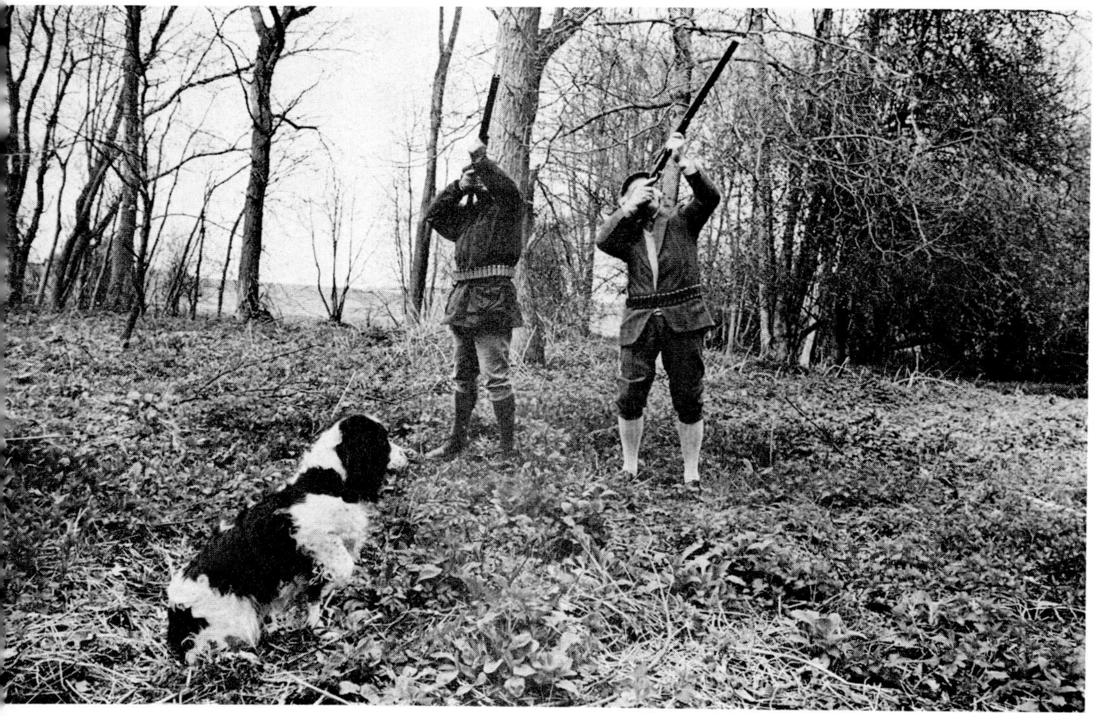

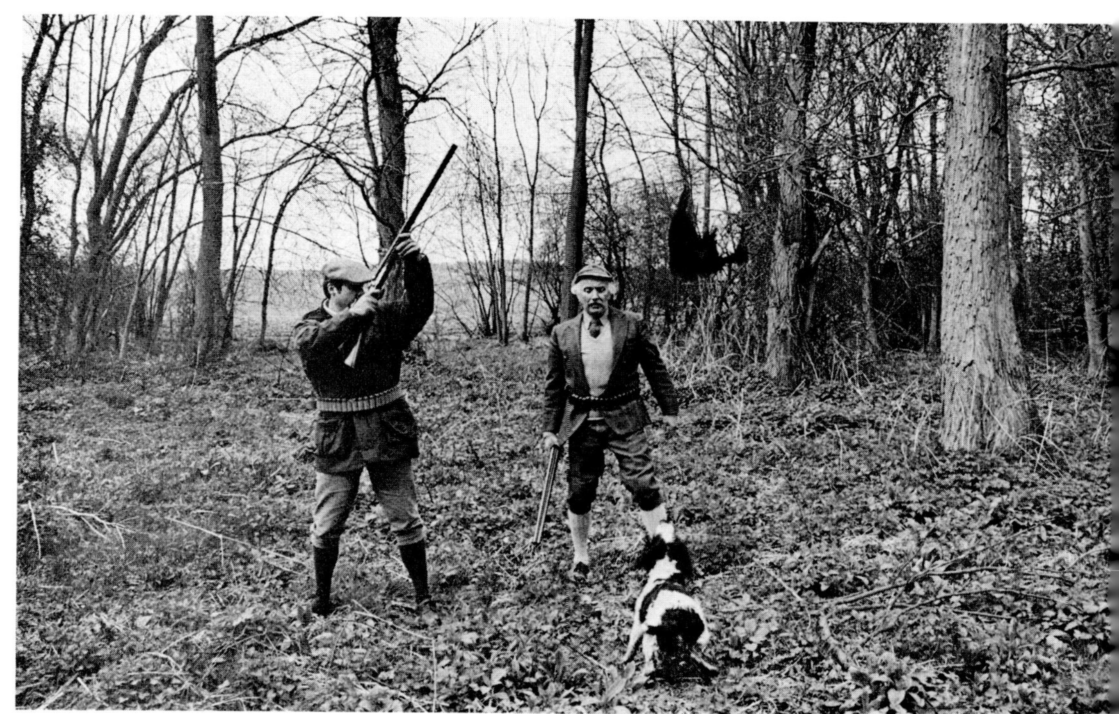

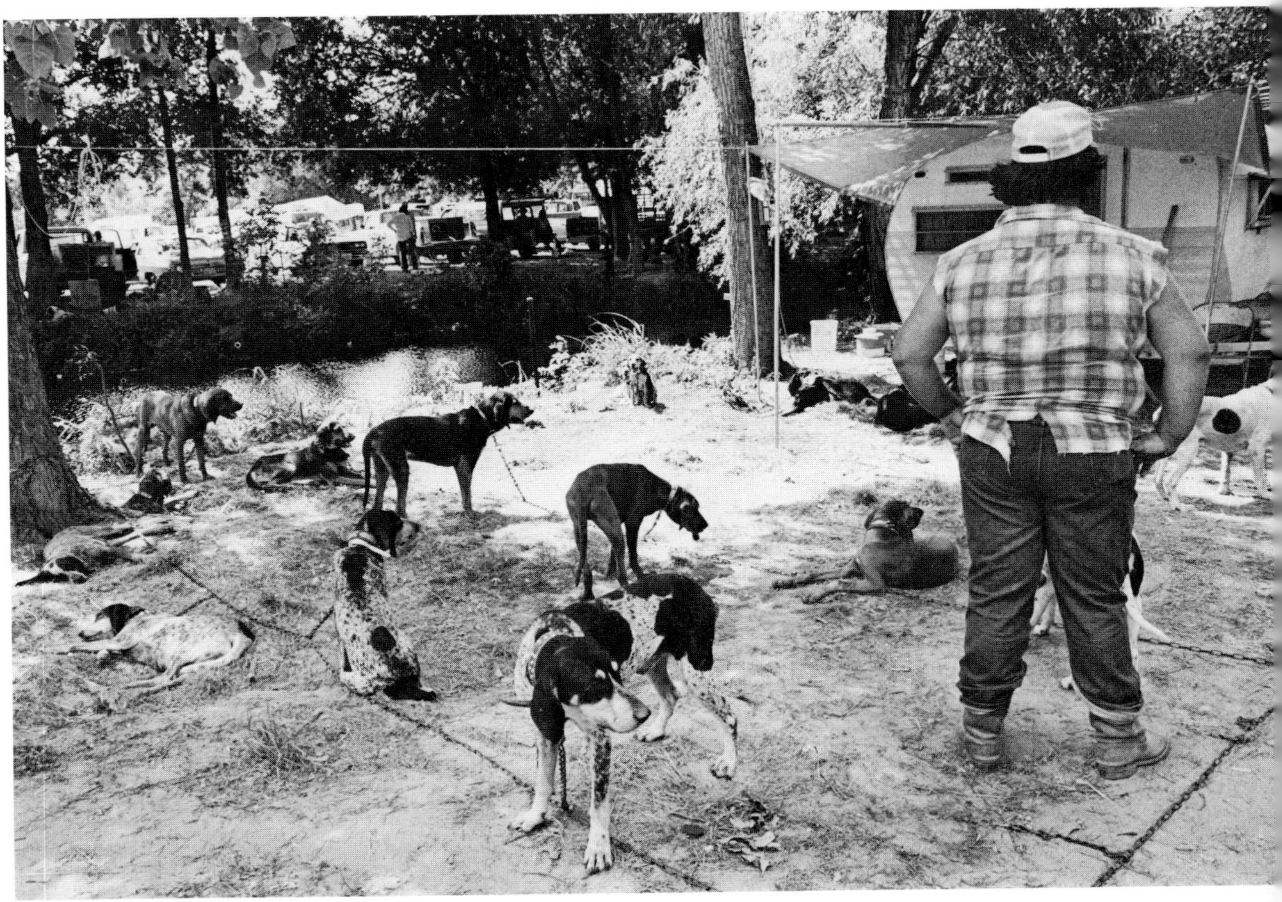

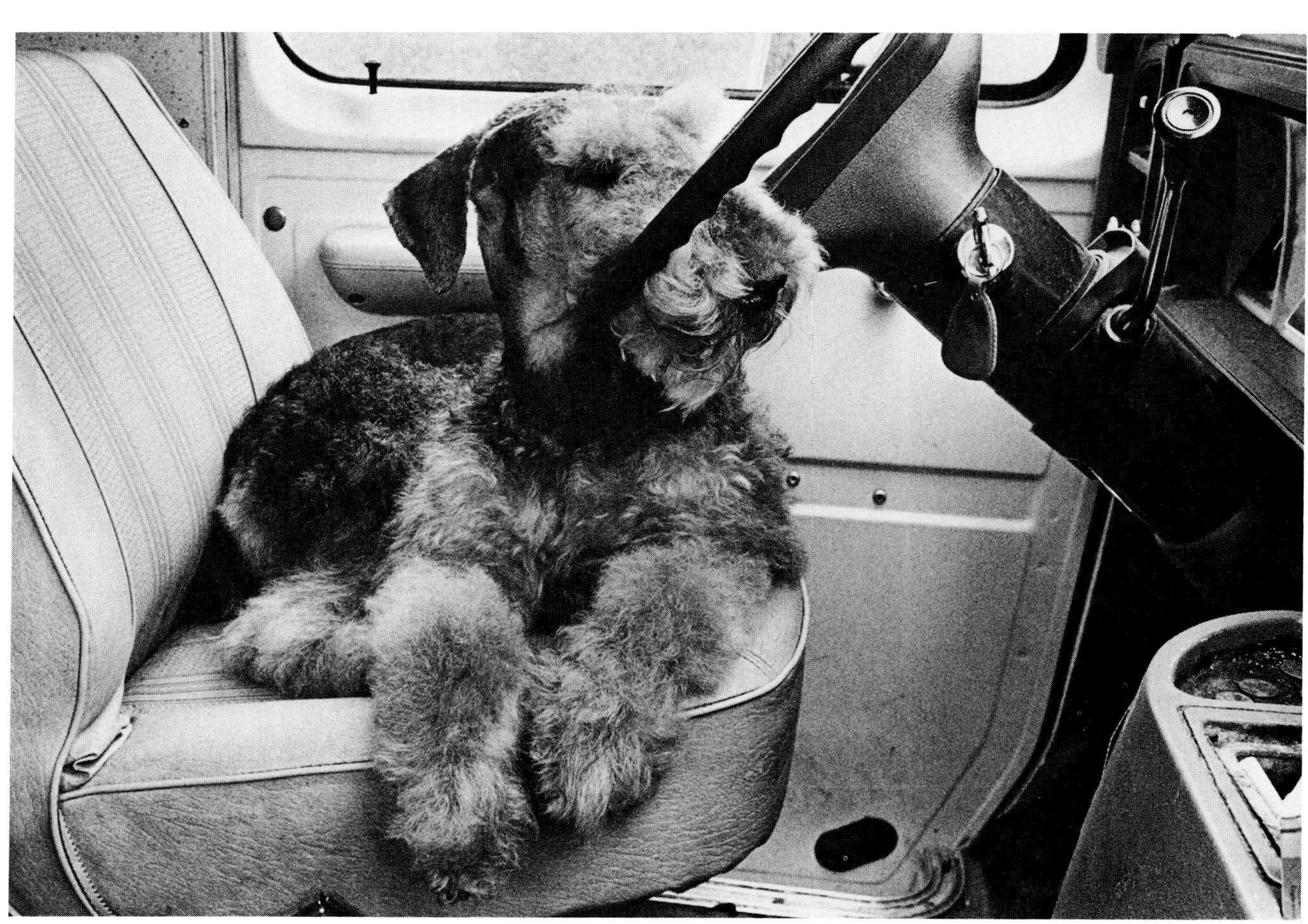

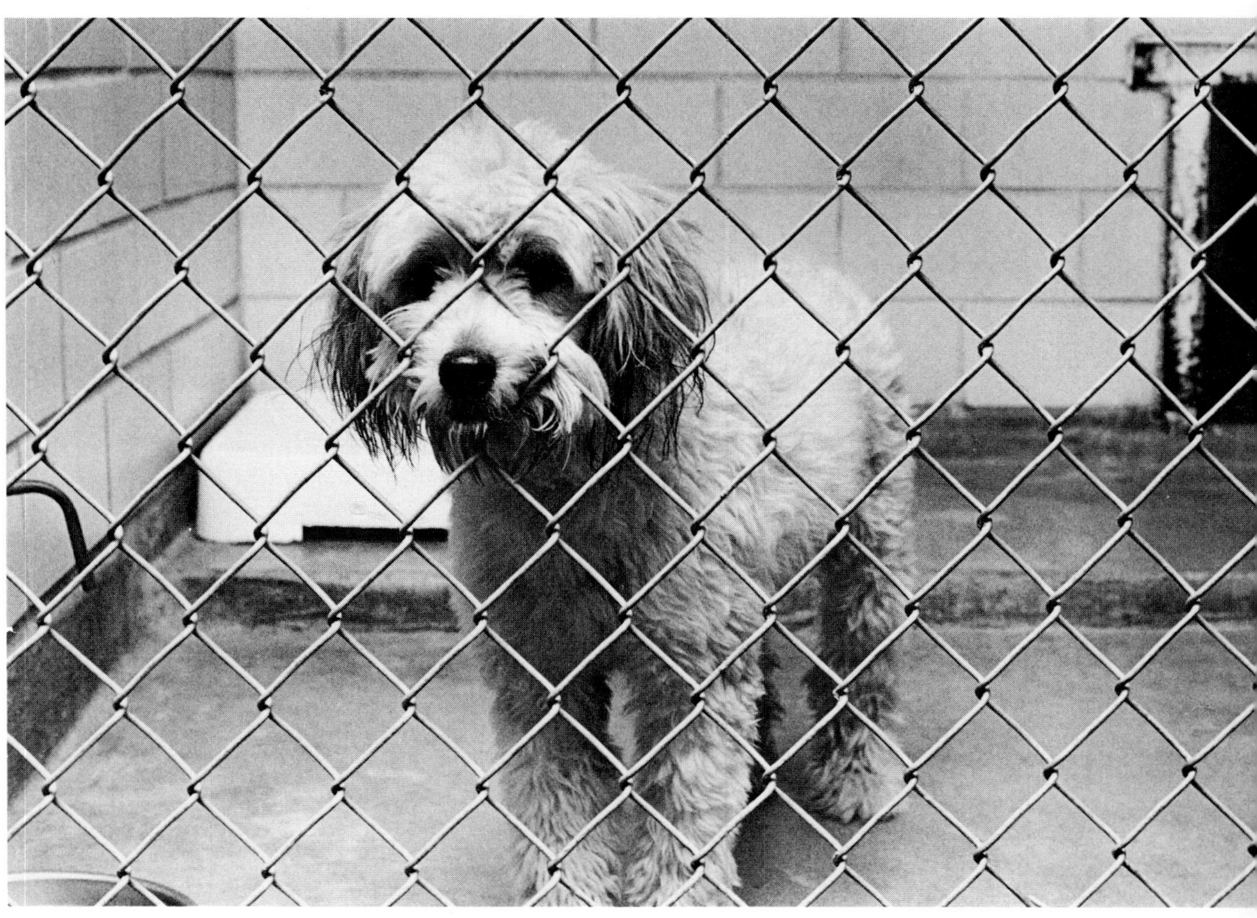

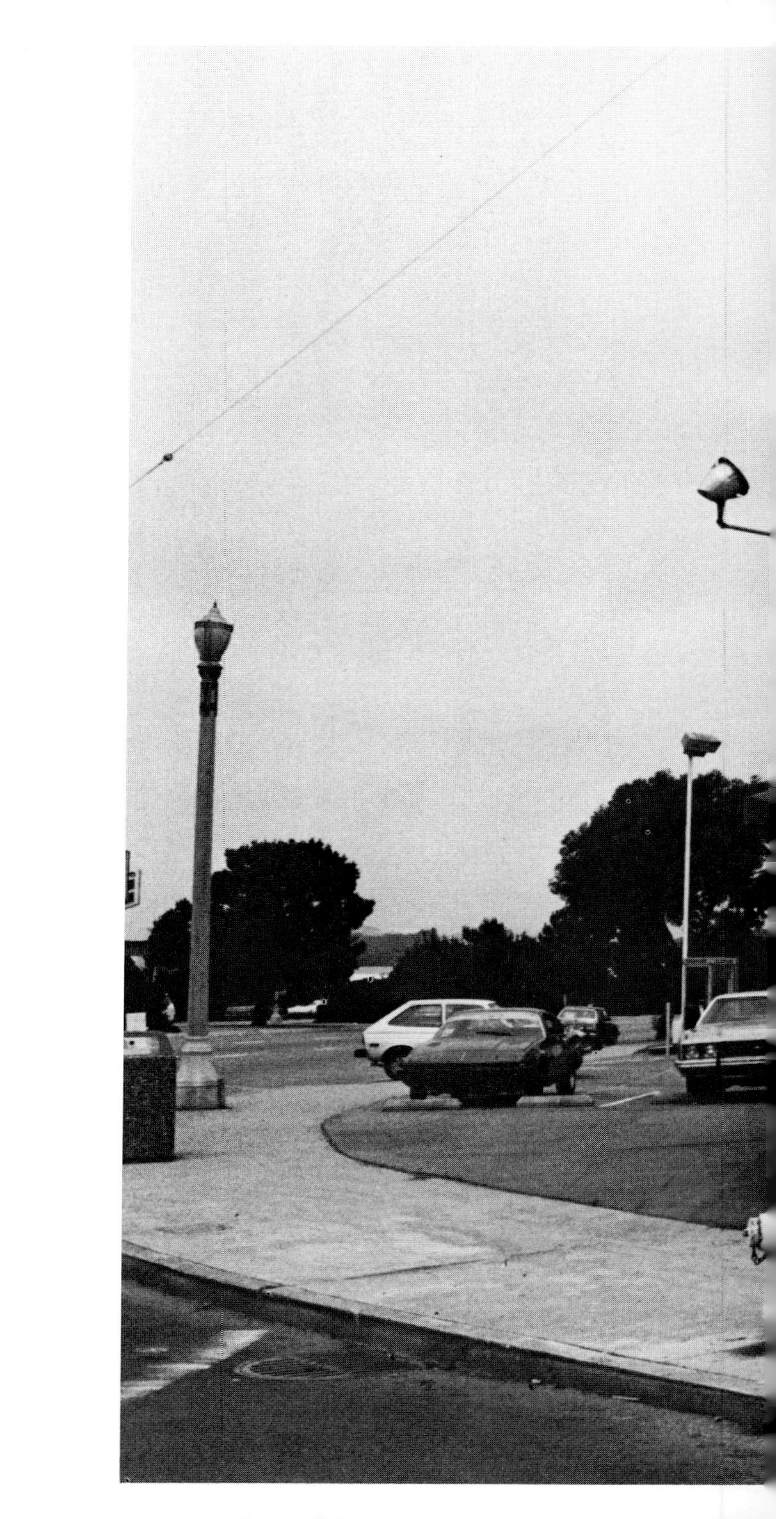

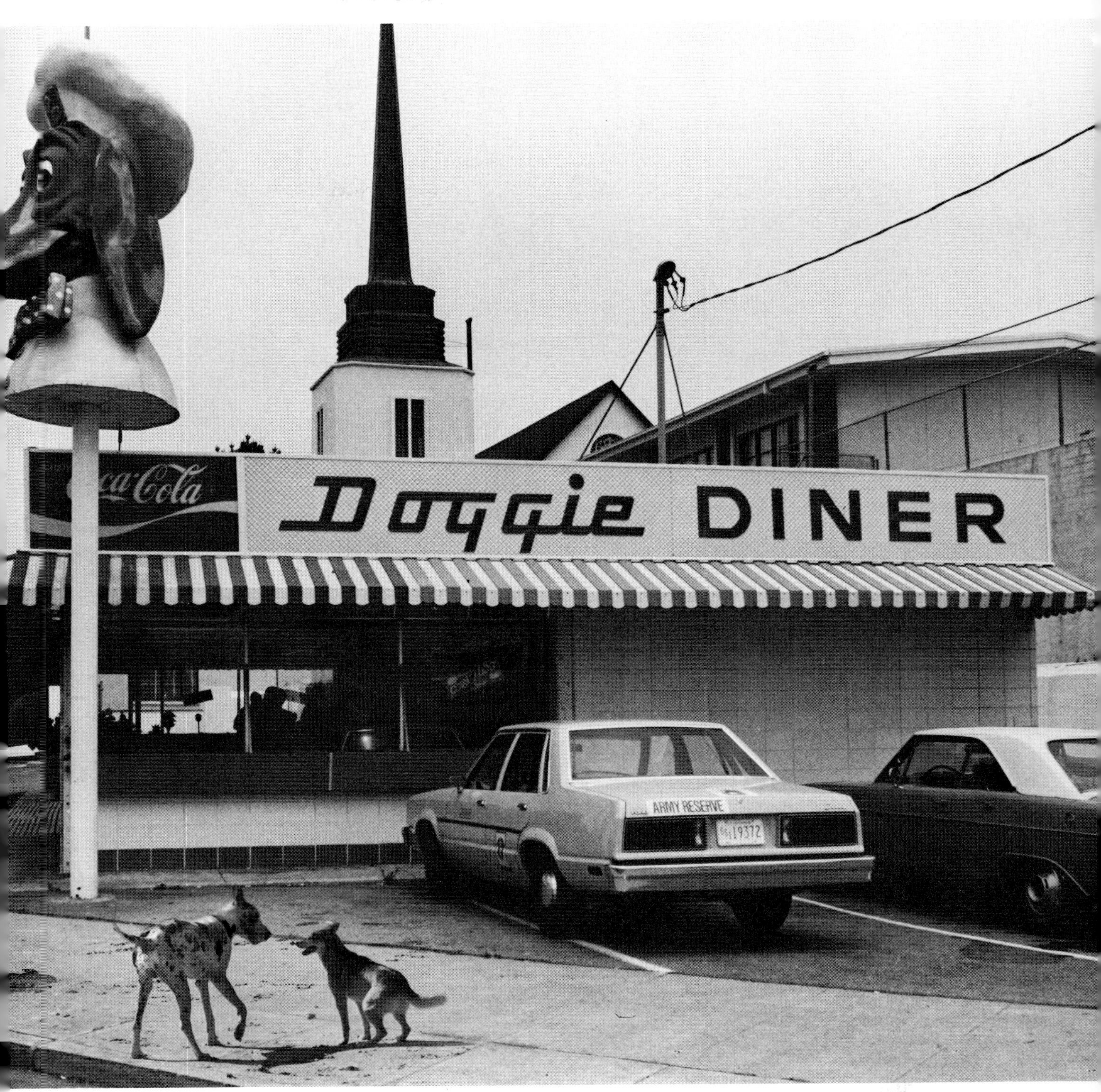
ca-Cola
Doggie DINER
ARMY RESERVE
19372

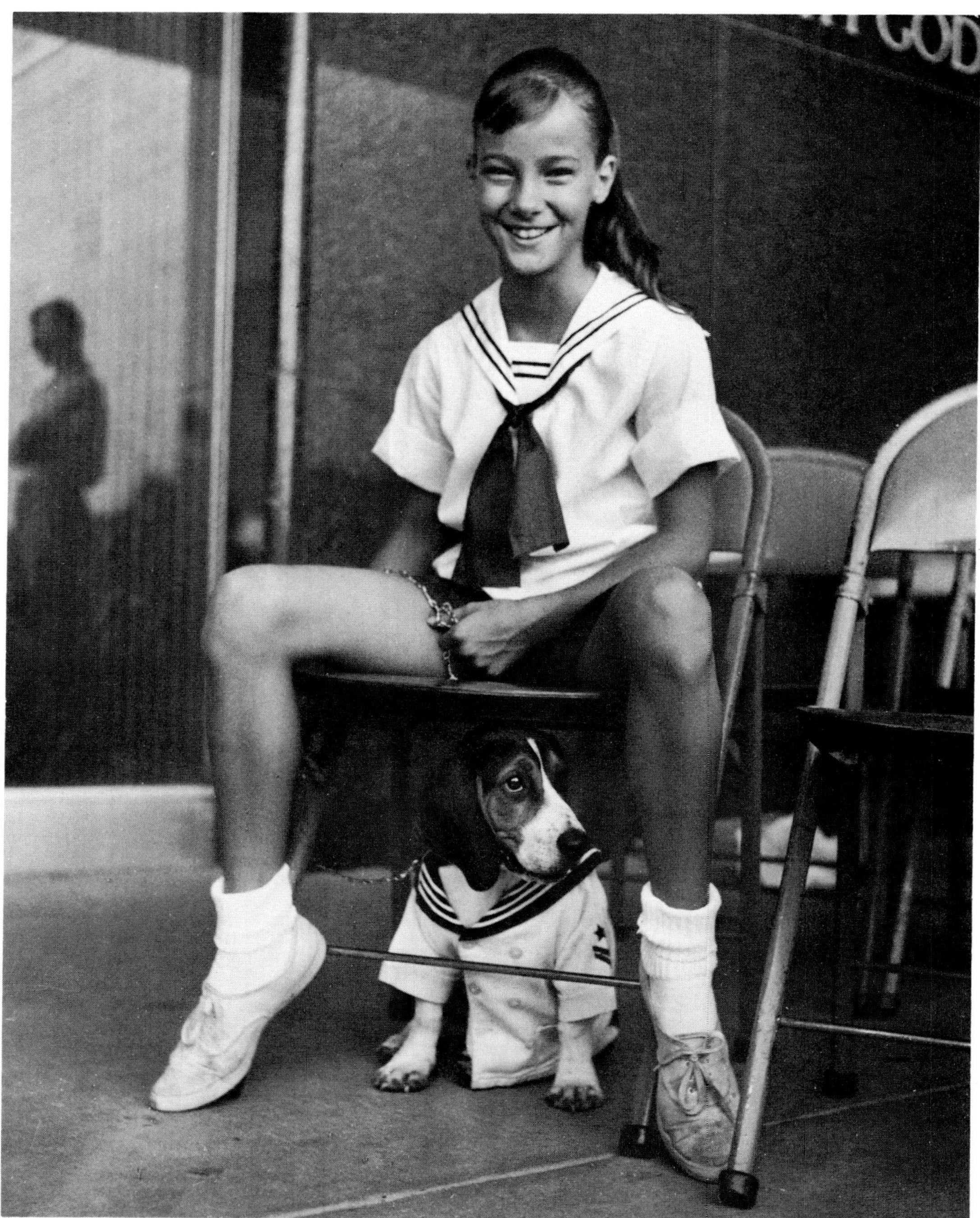

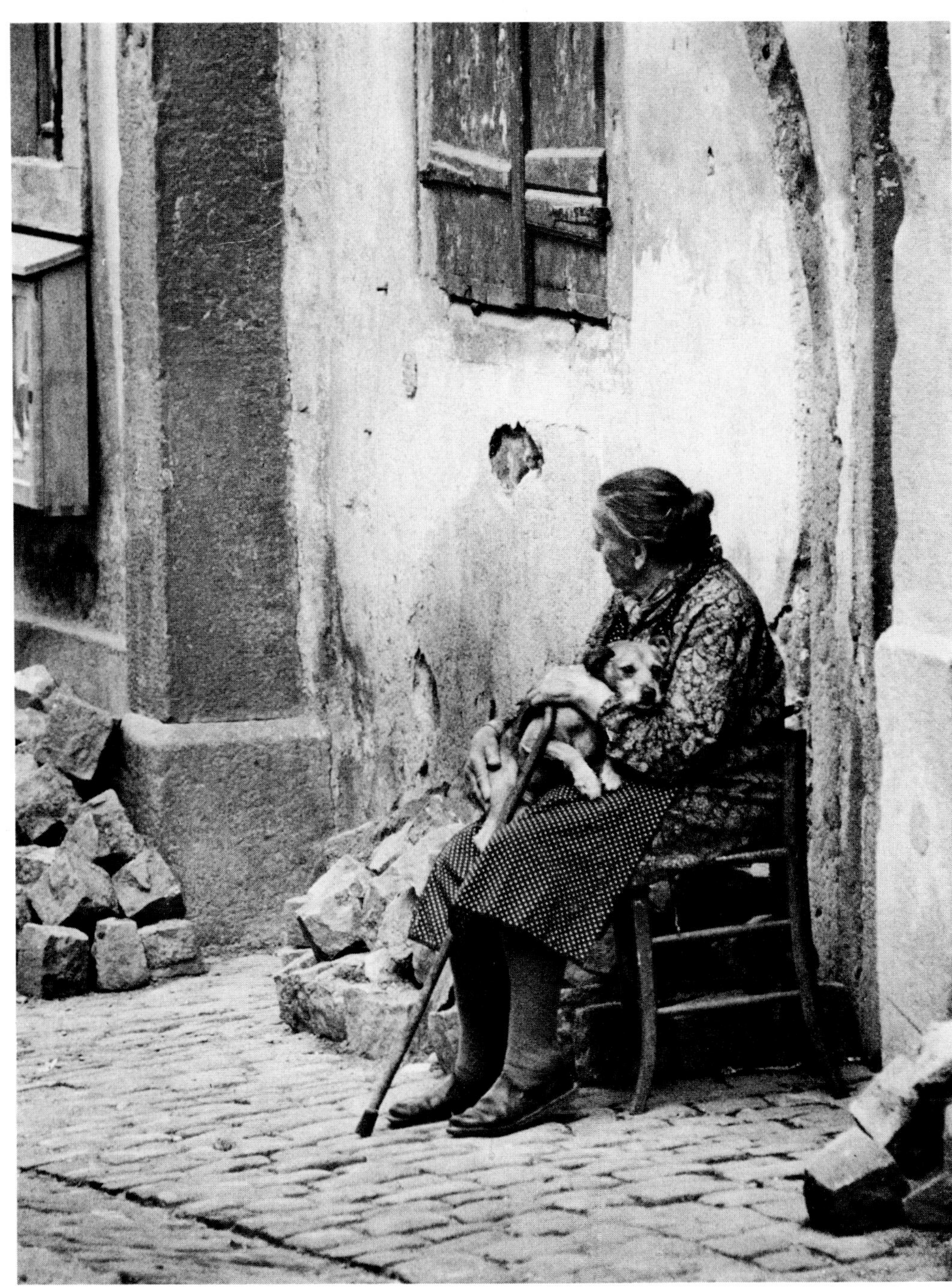

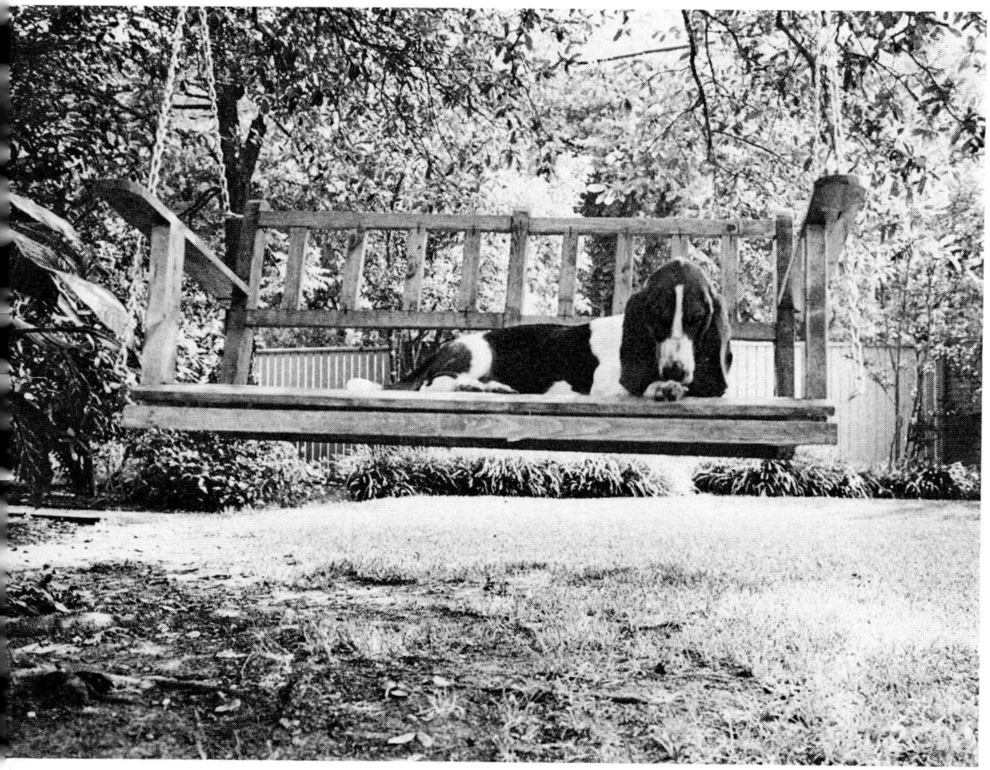

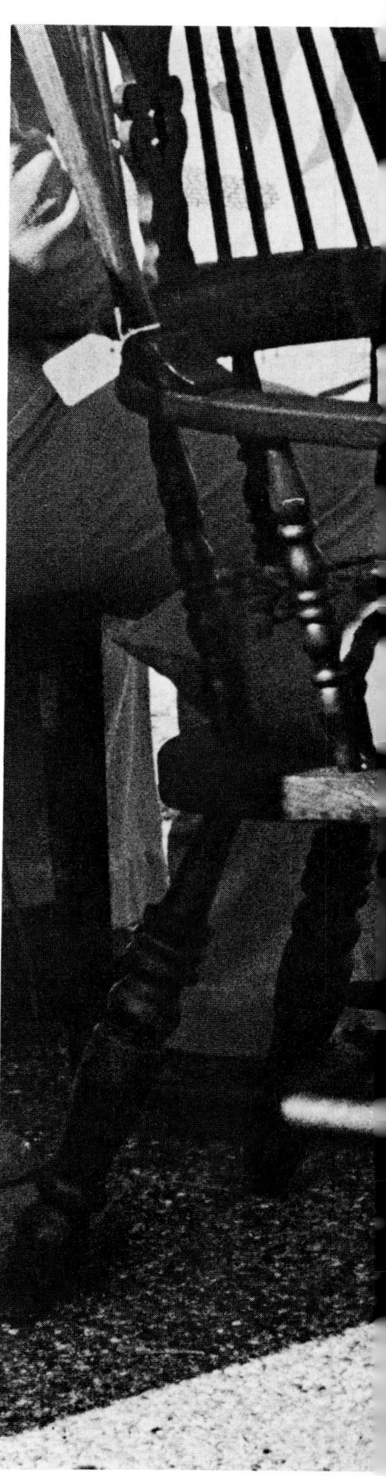

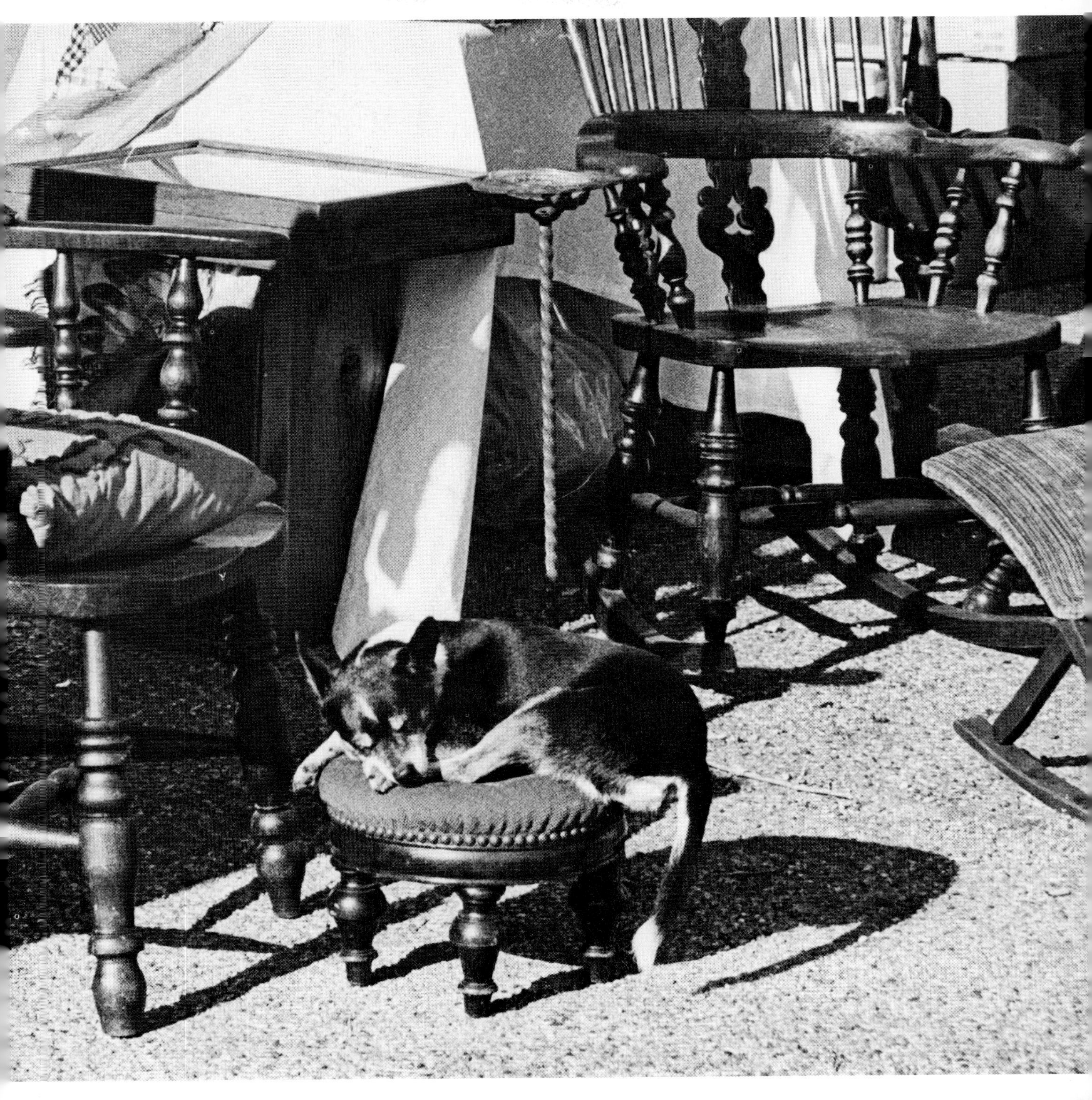

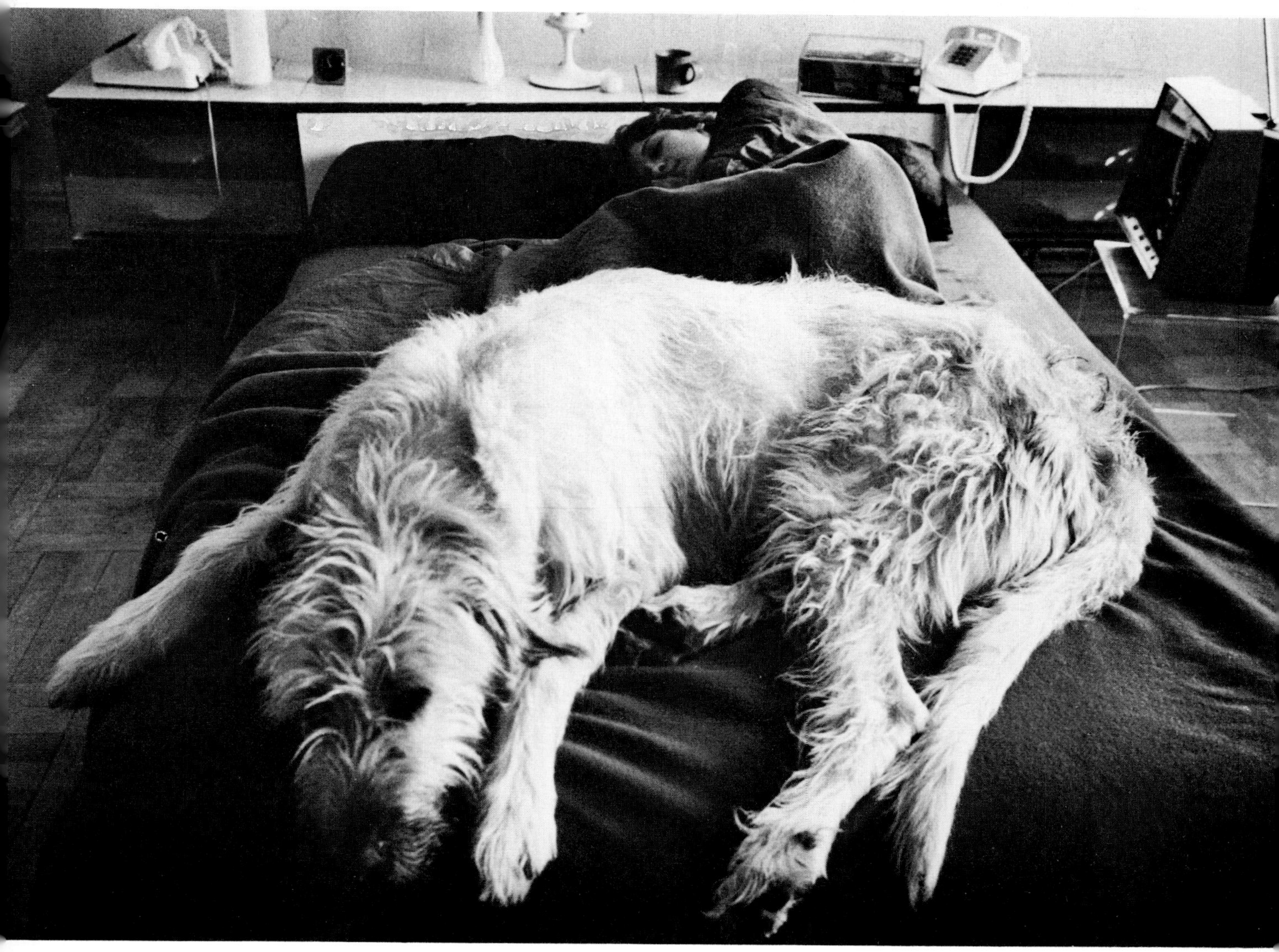

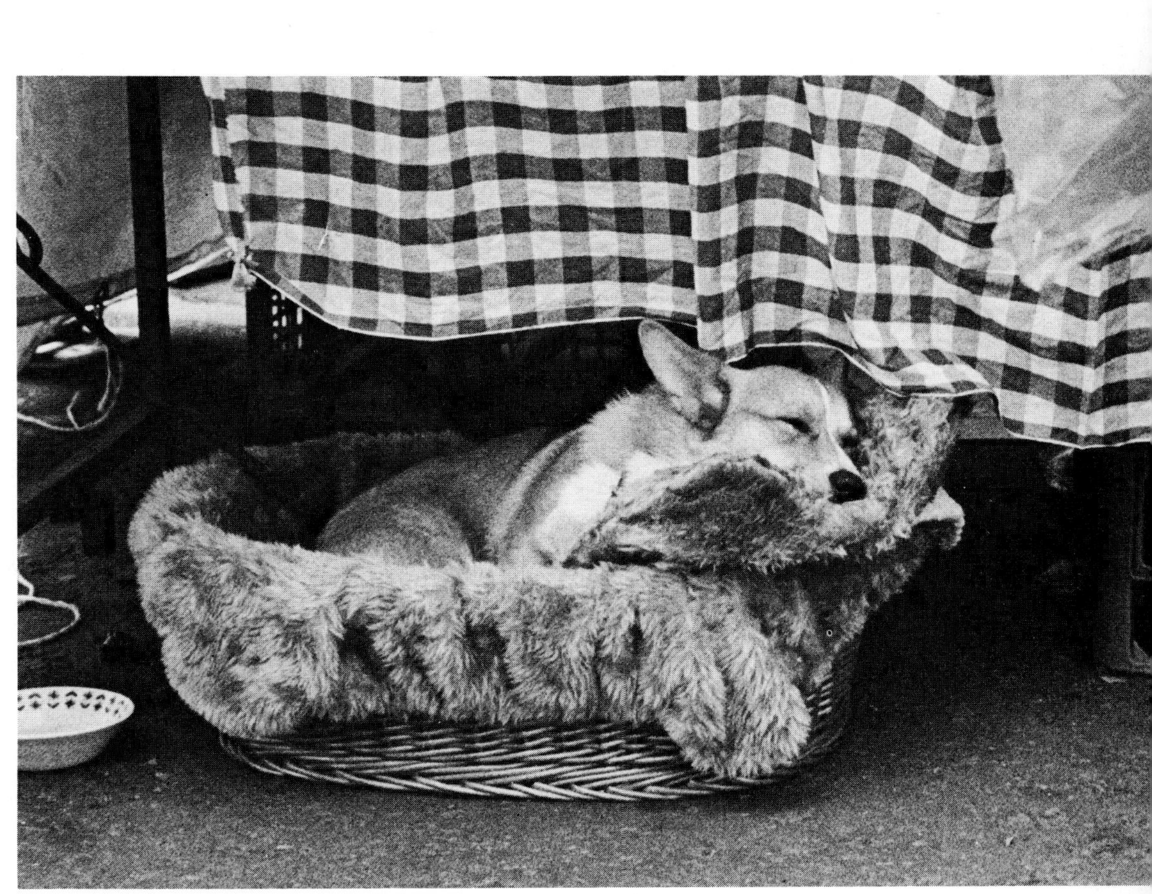

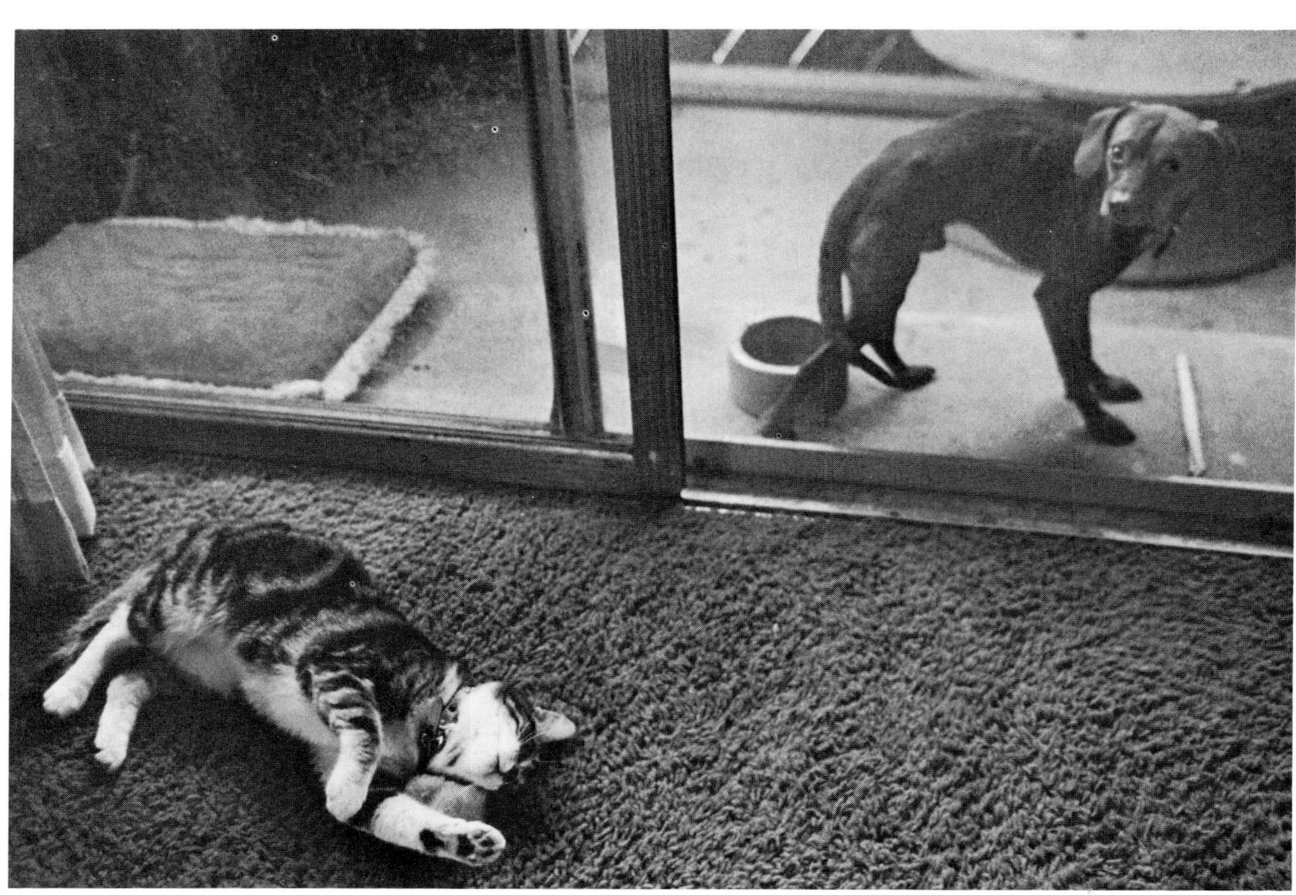

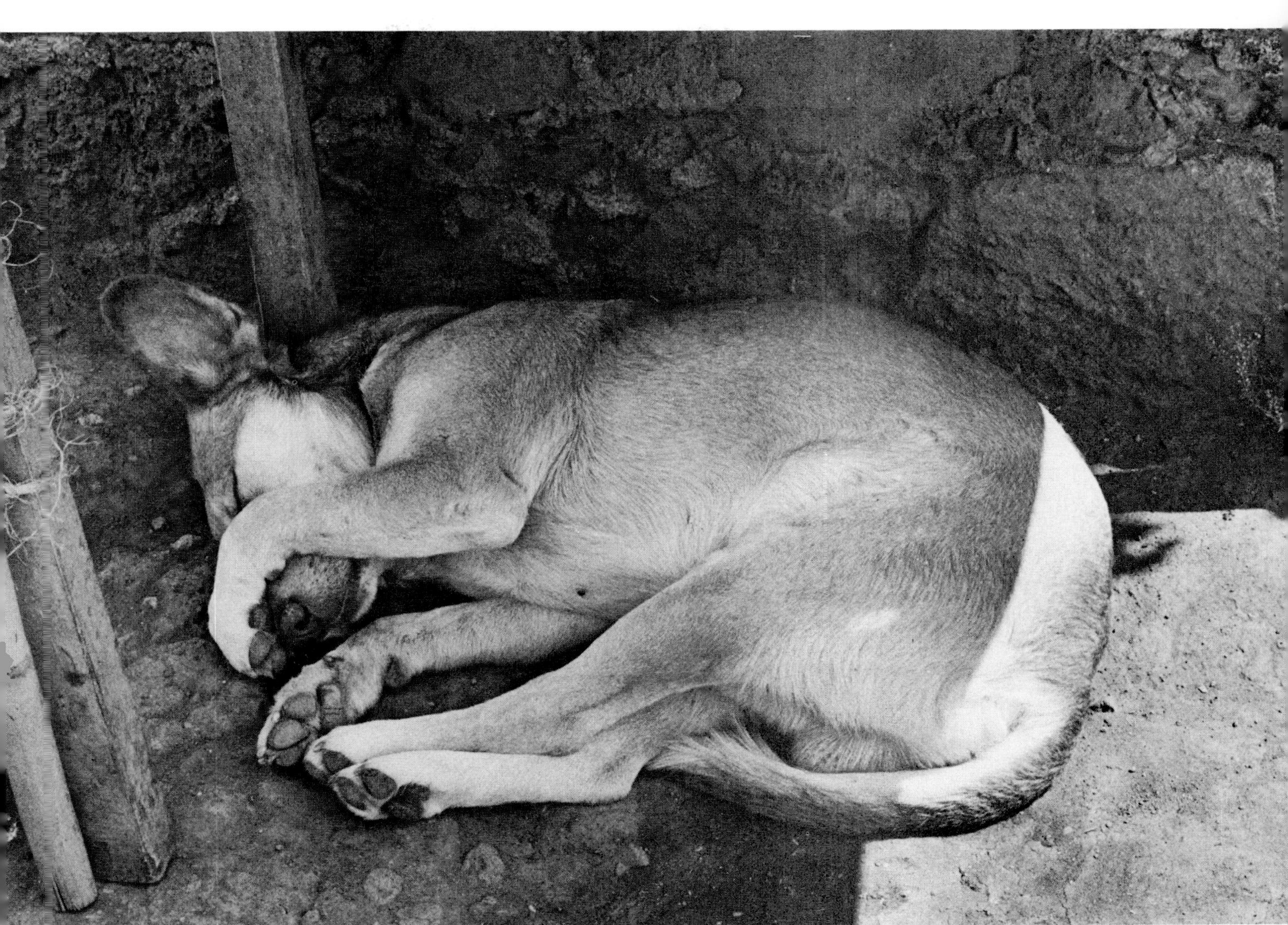

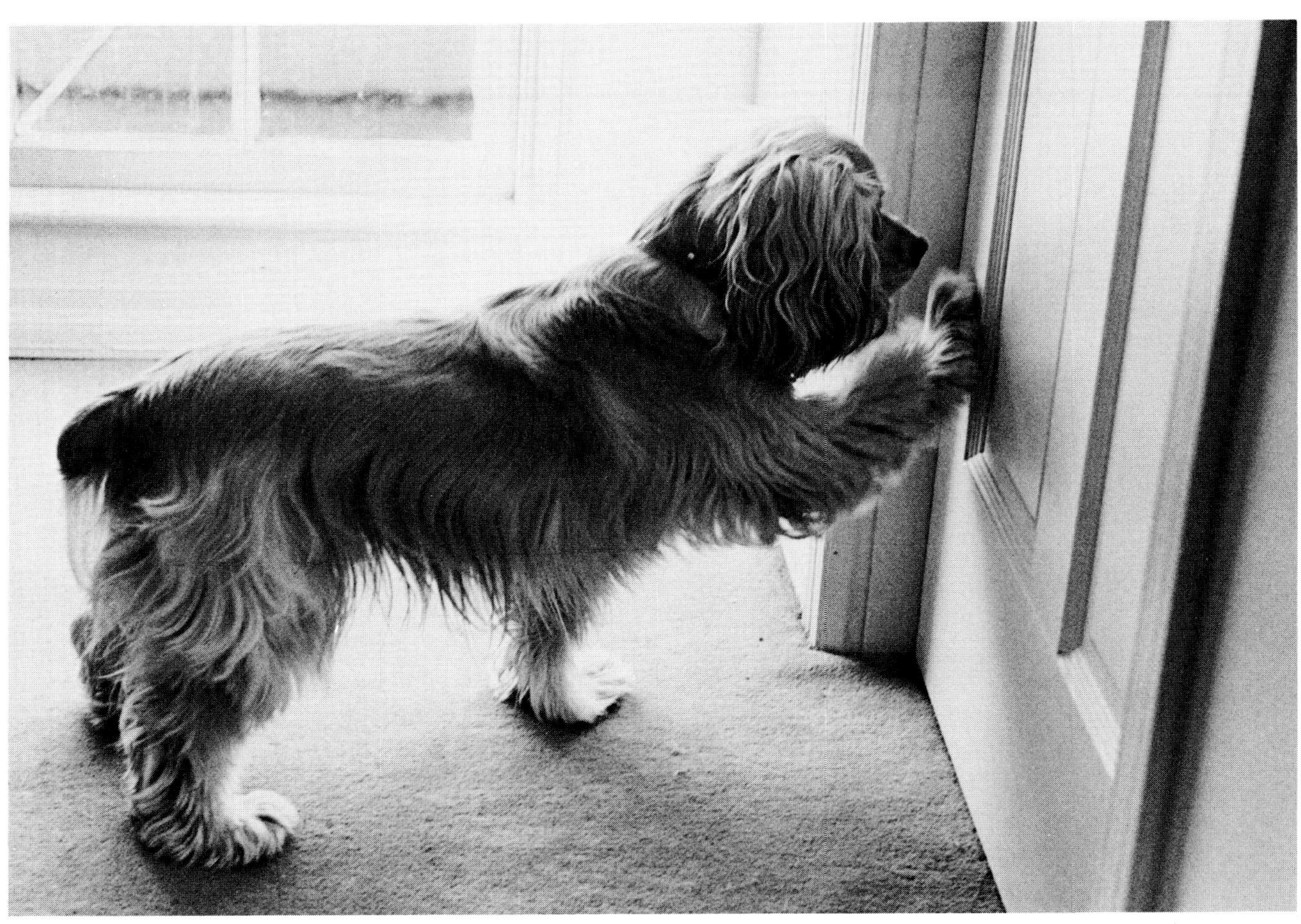

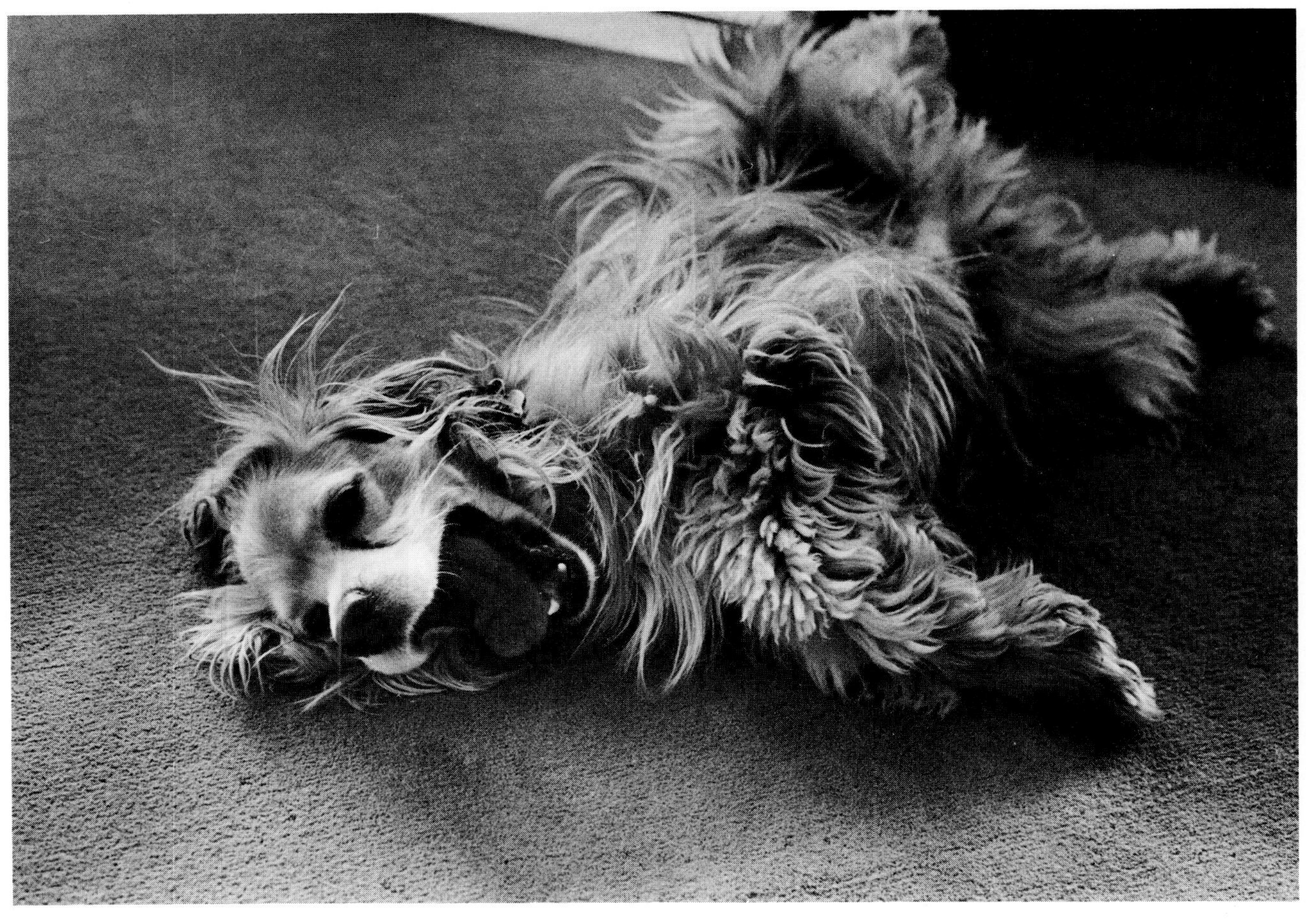

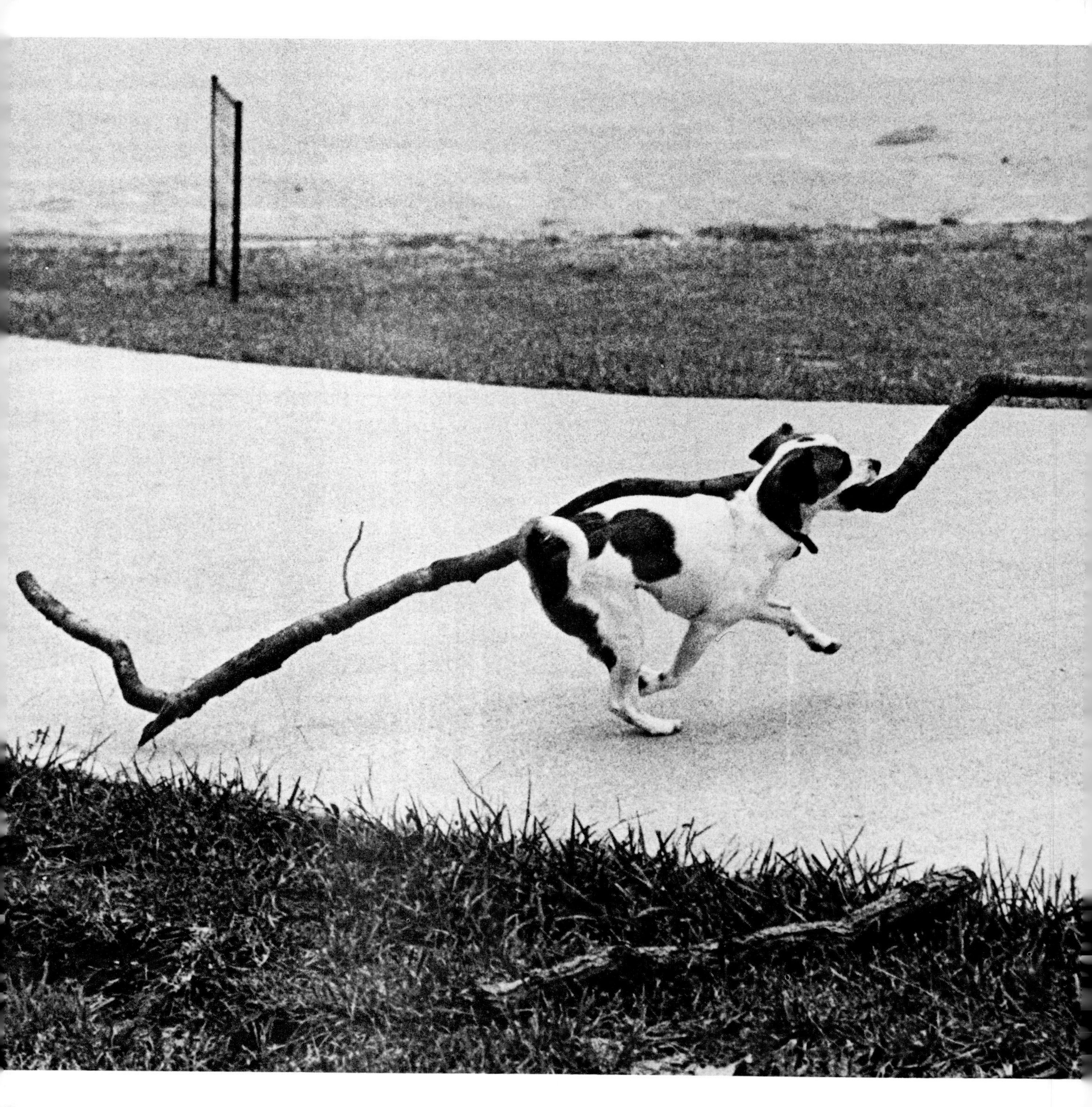

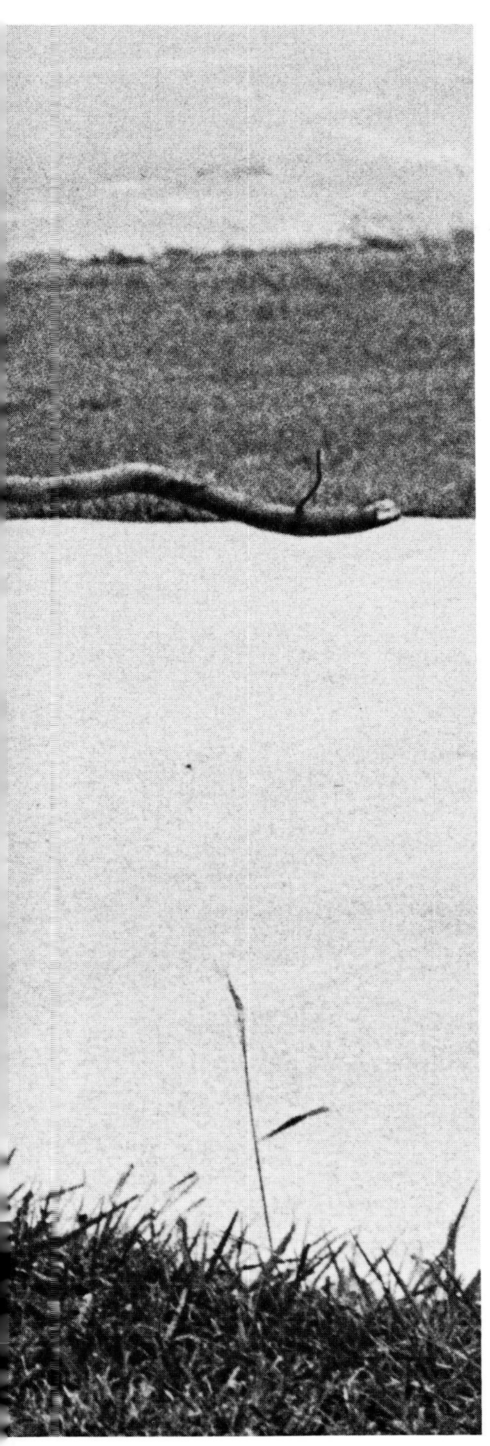

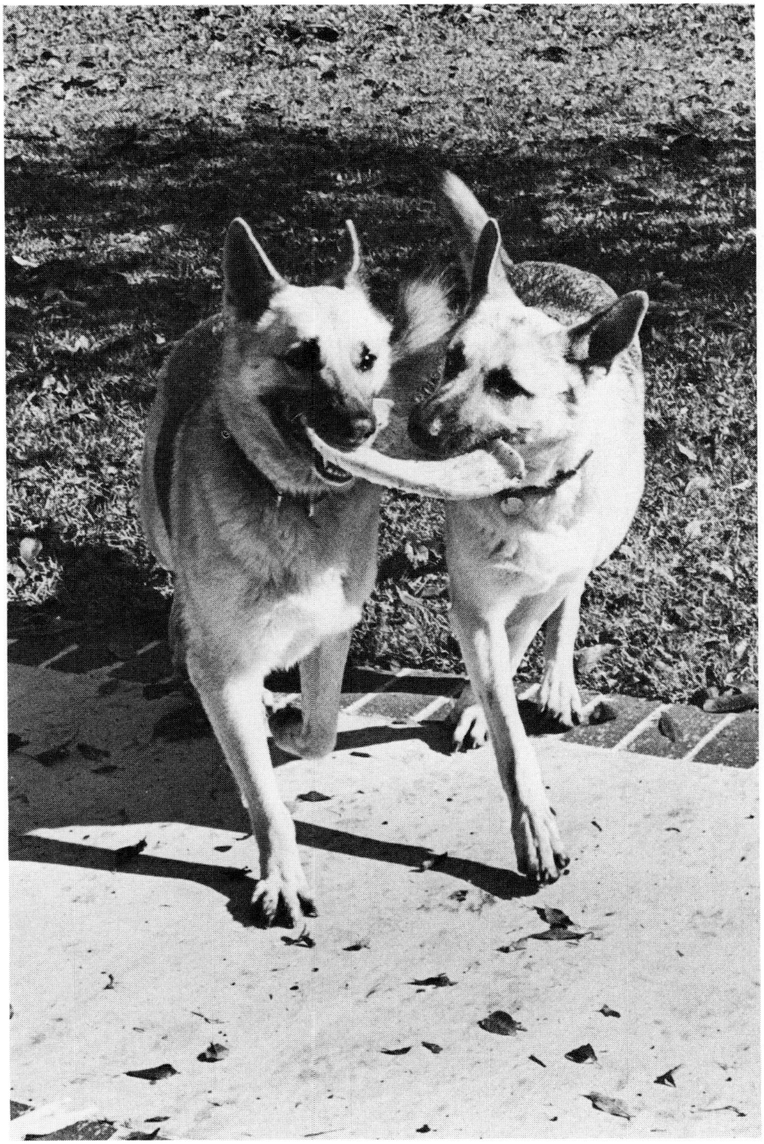

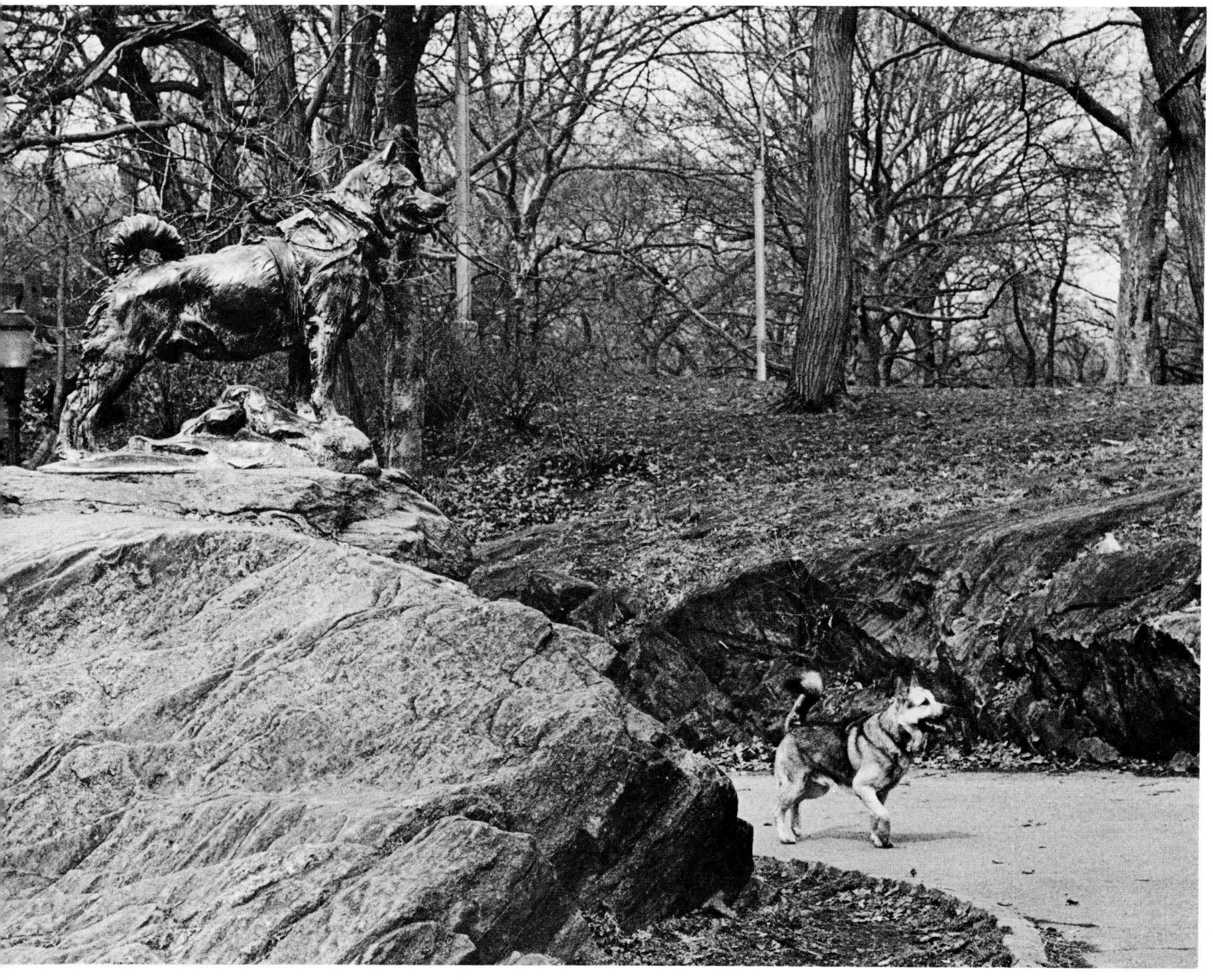

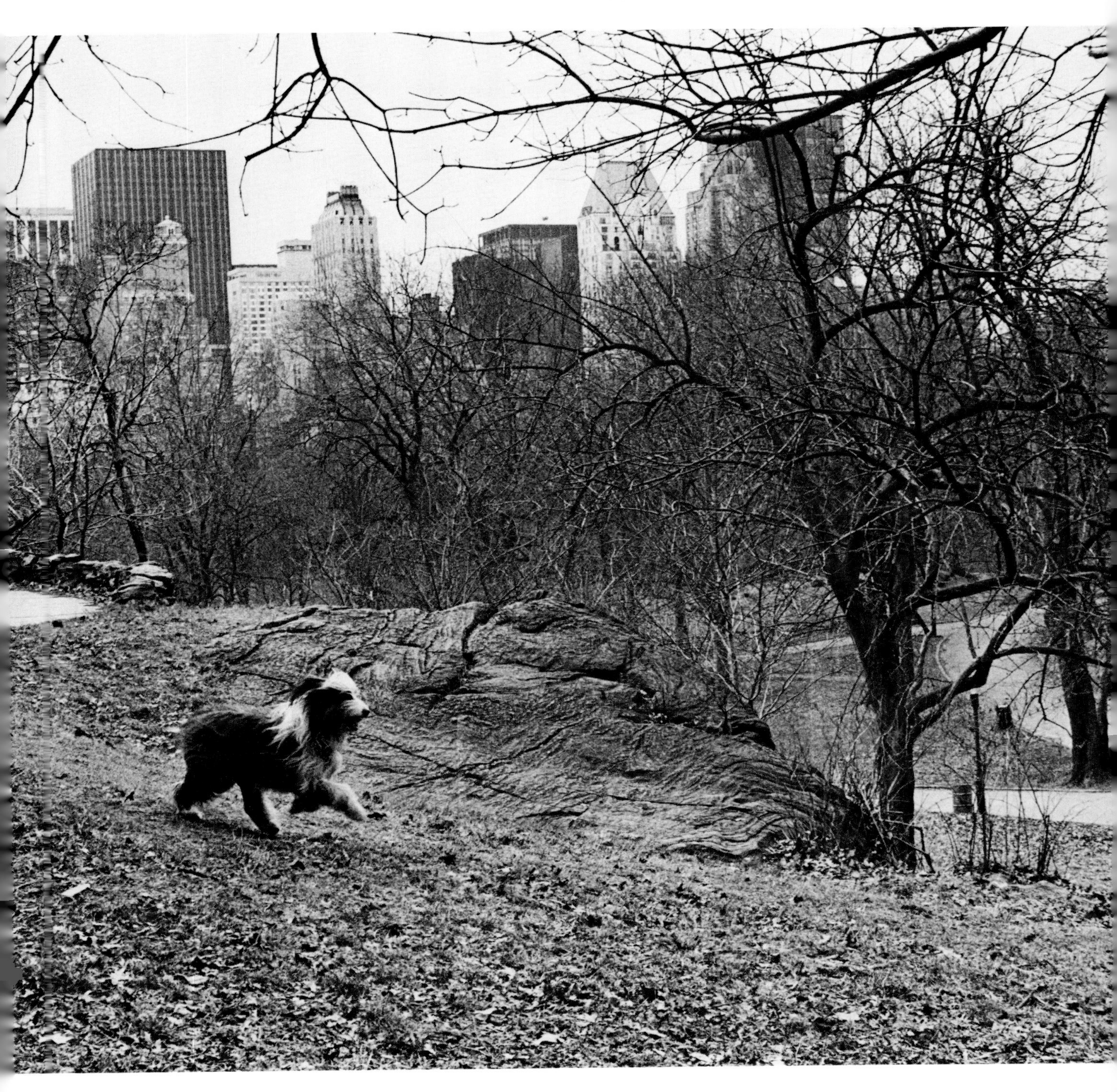

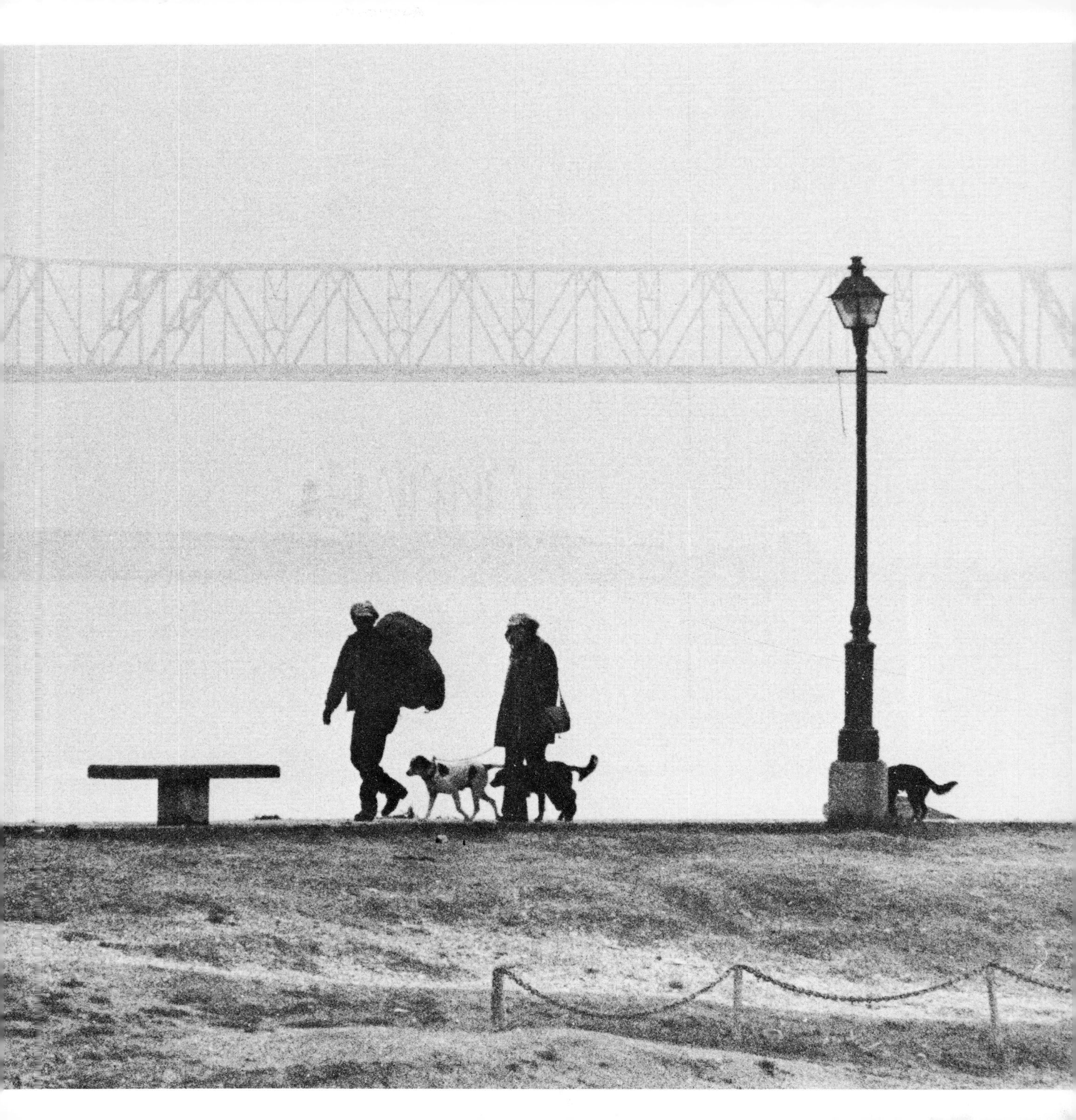

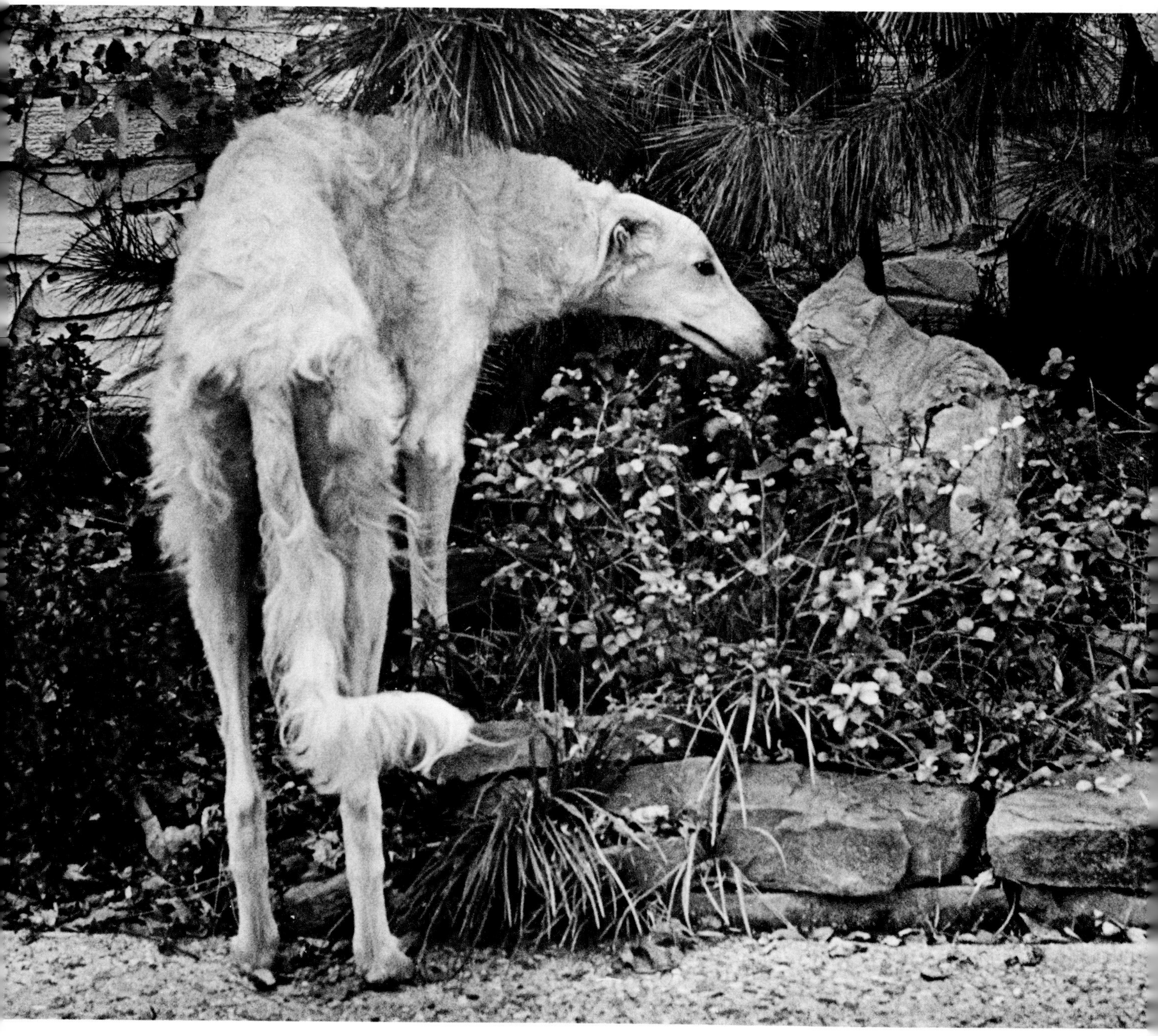

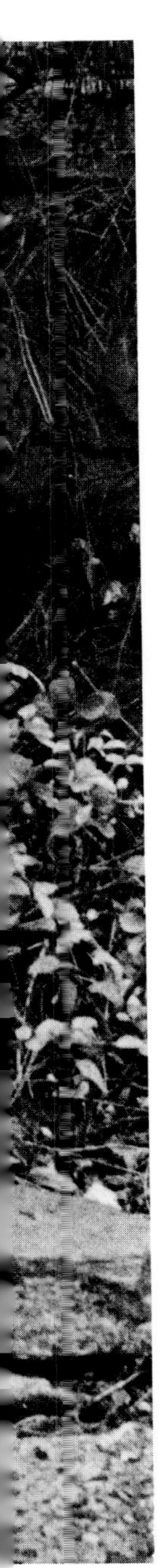

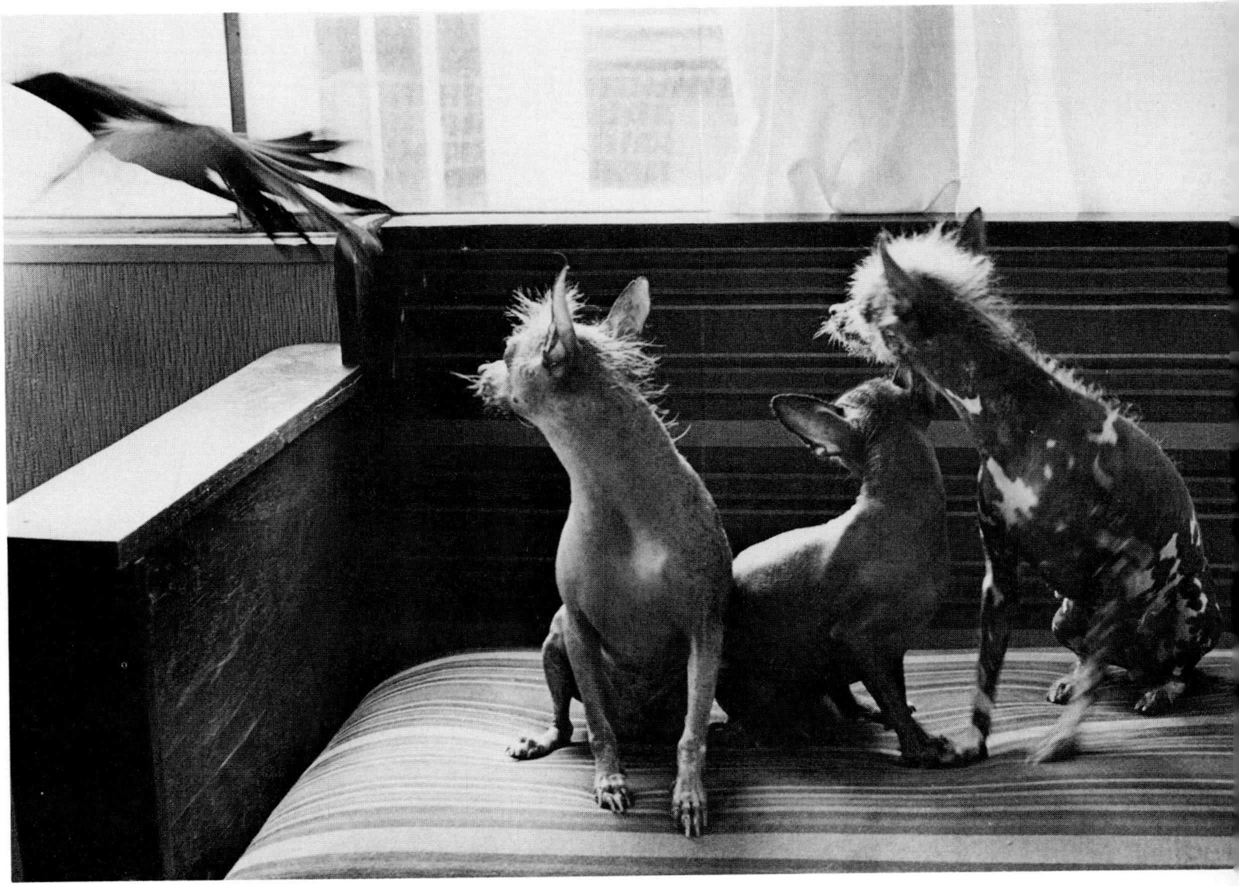

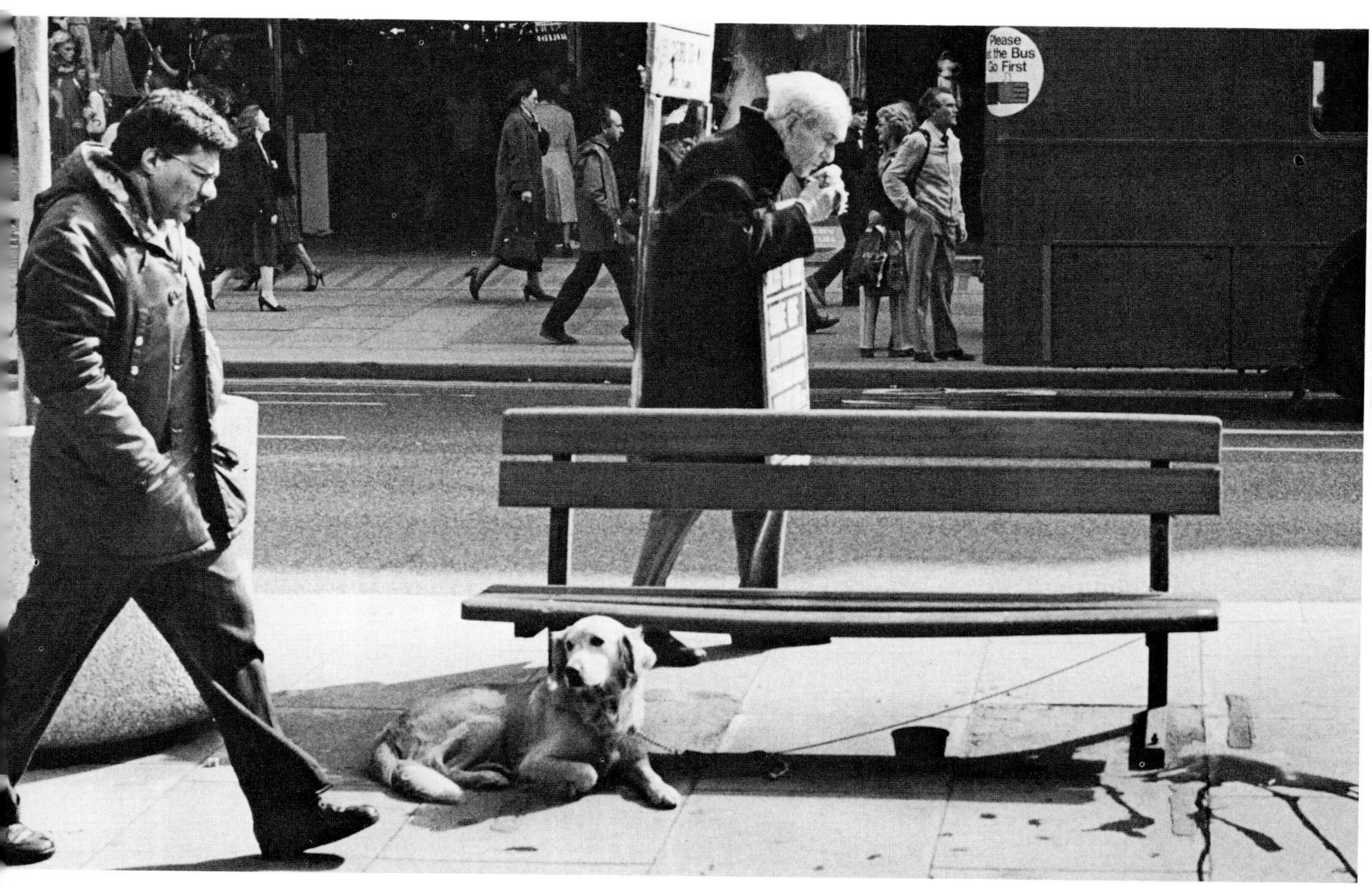

Please
t the Bus
Go First

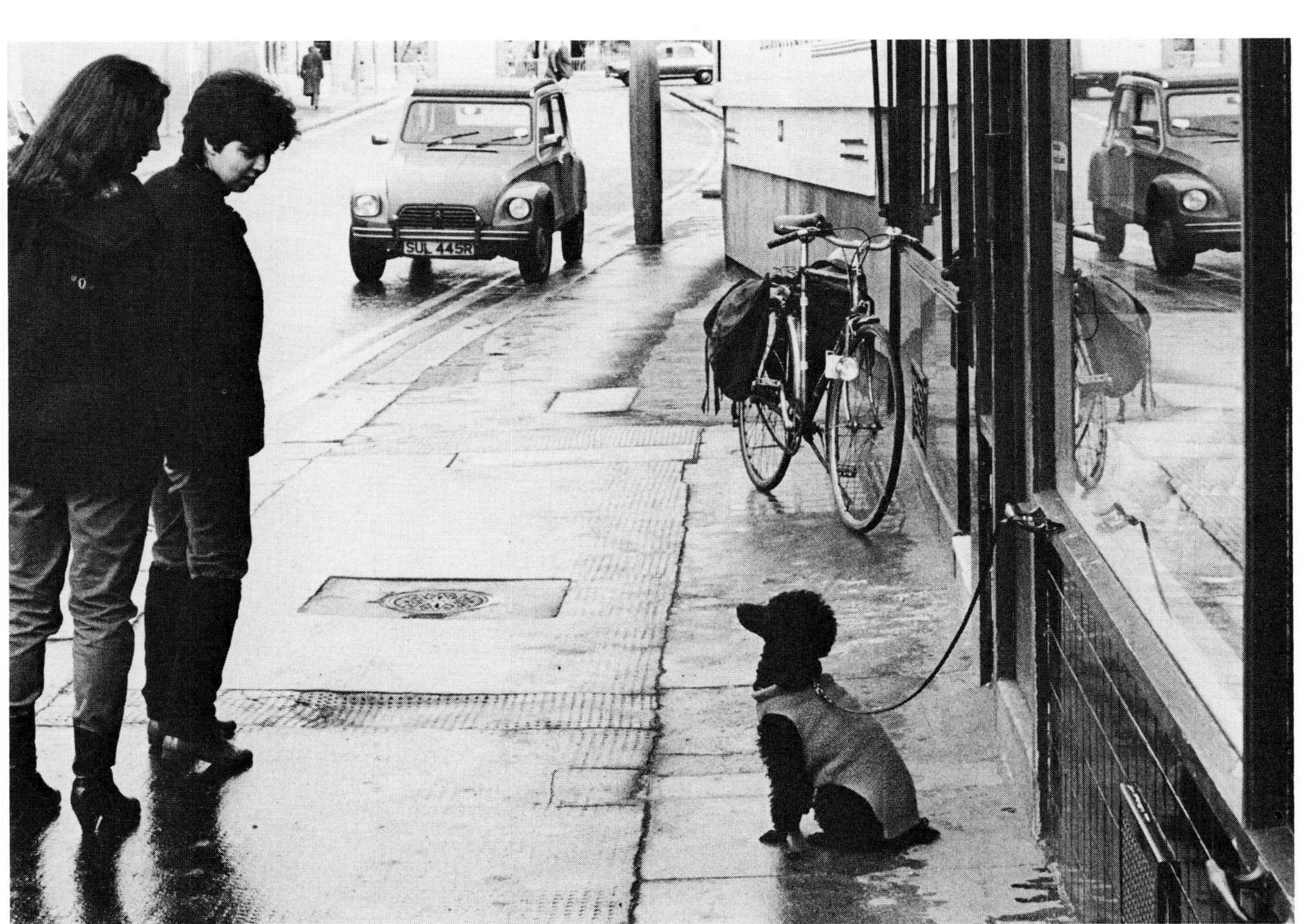
SUL 445R

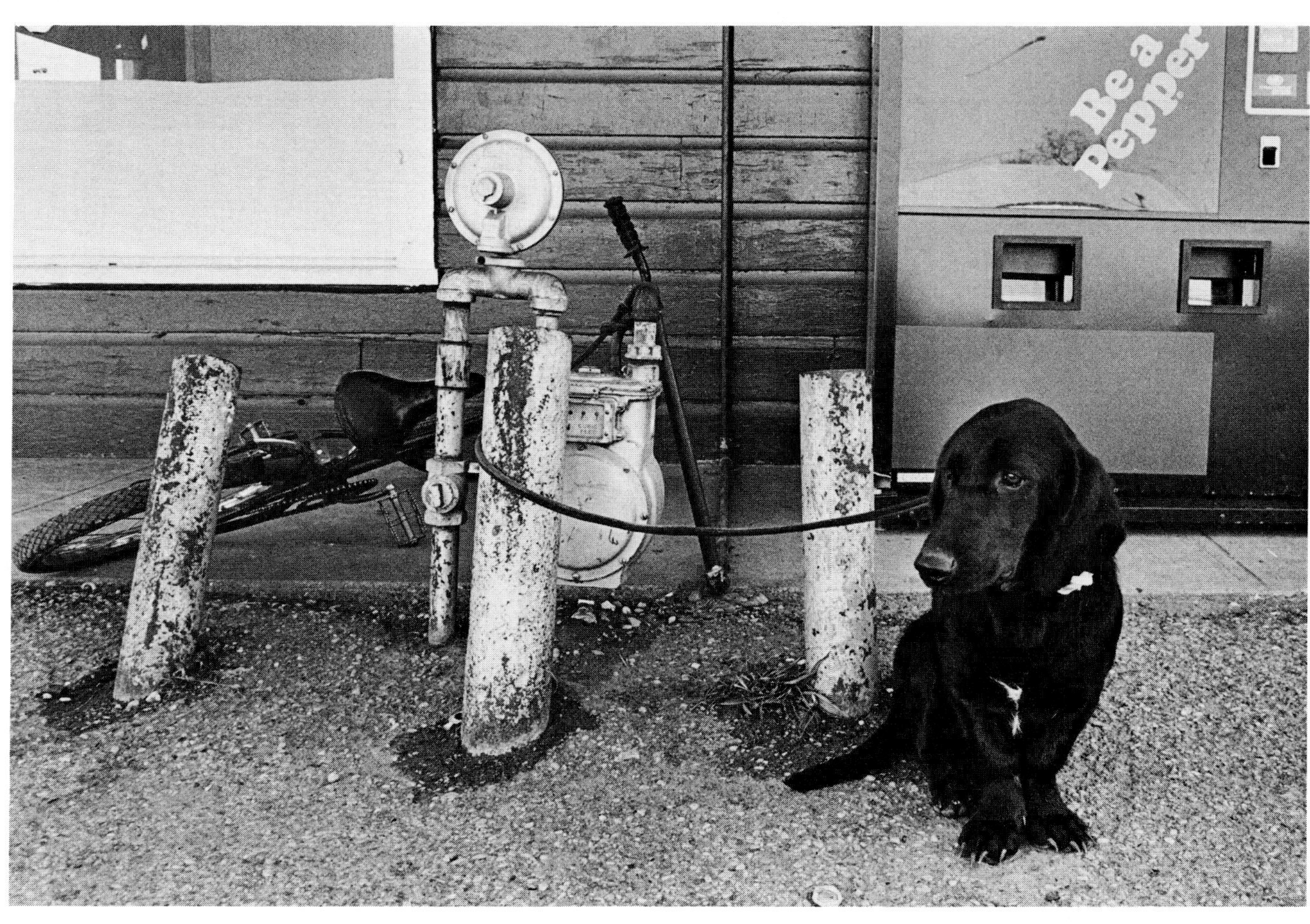
Be a

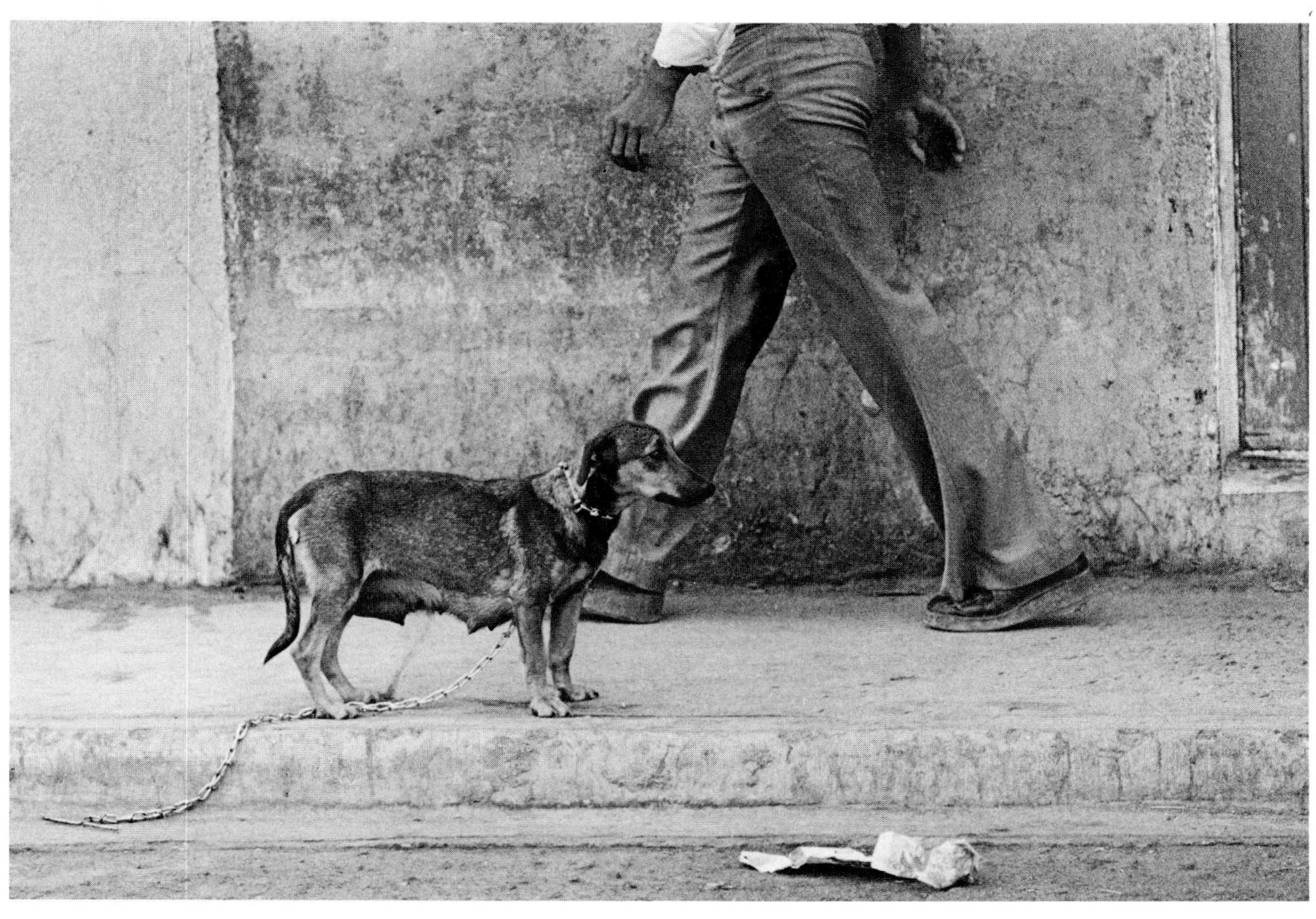

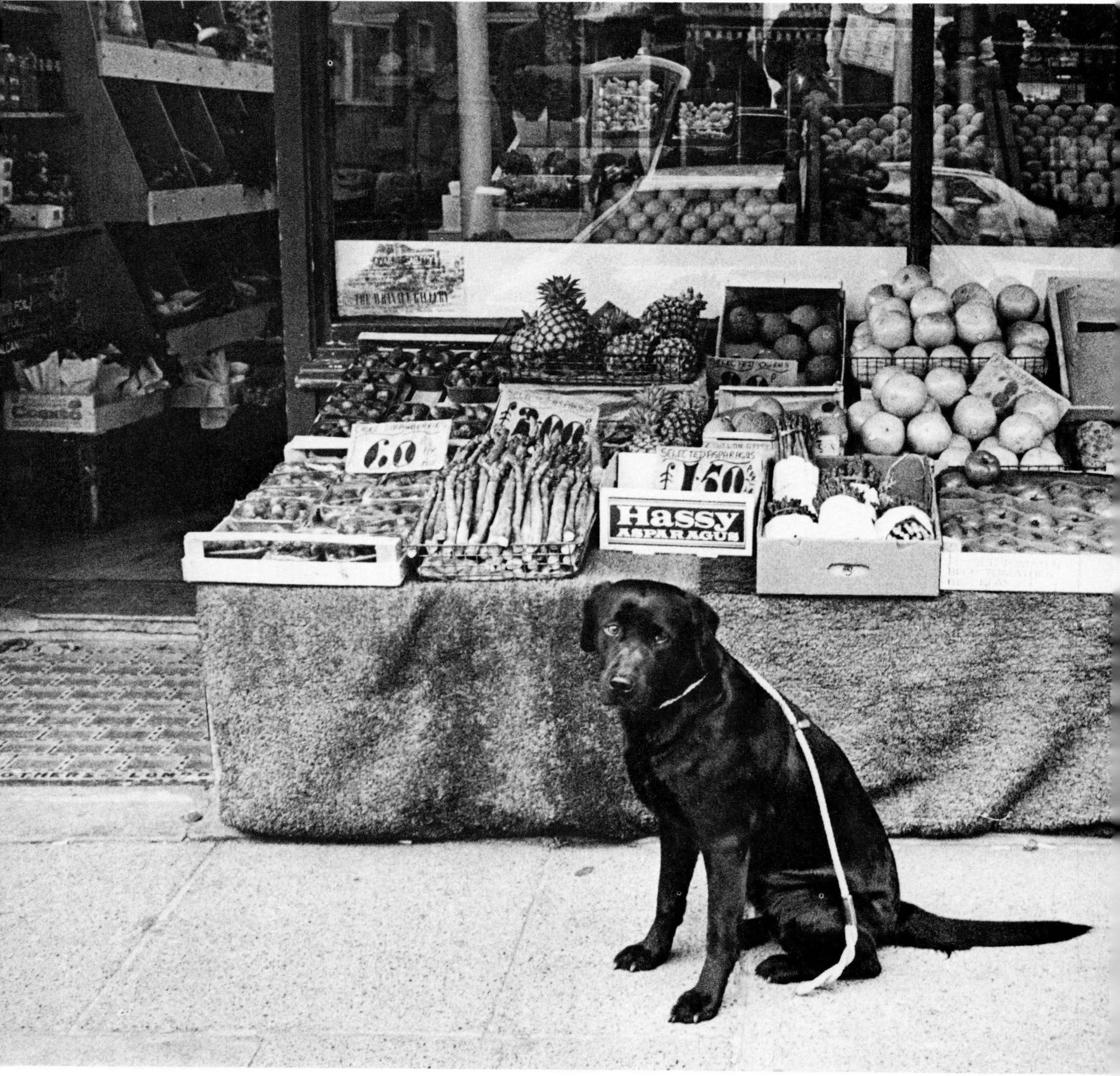
SELECTED ASPARAGUS
£1.50
Hassy
ASPARAGUS

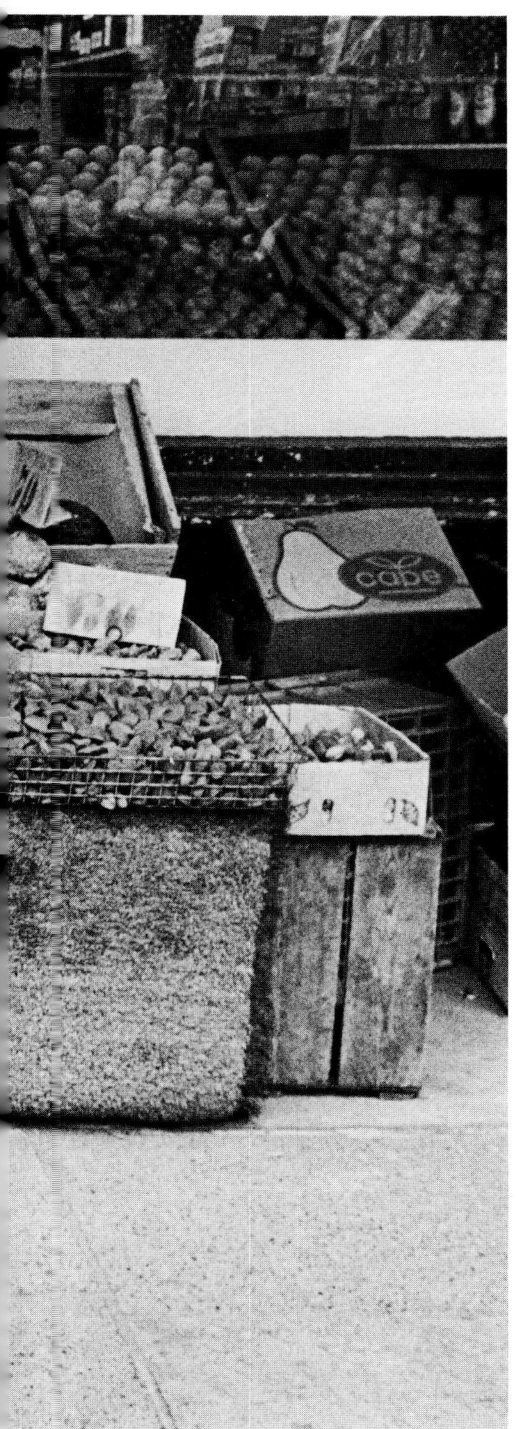
cape

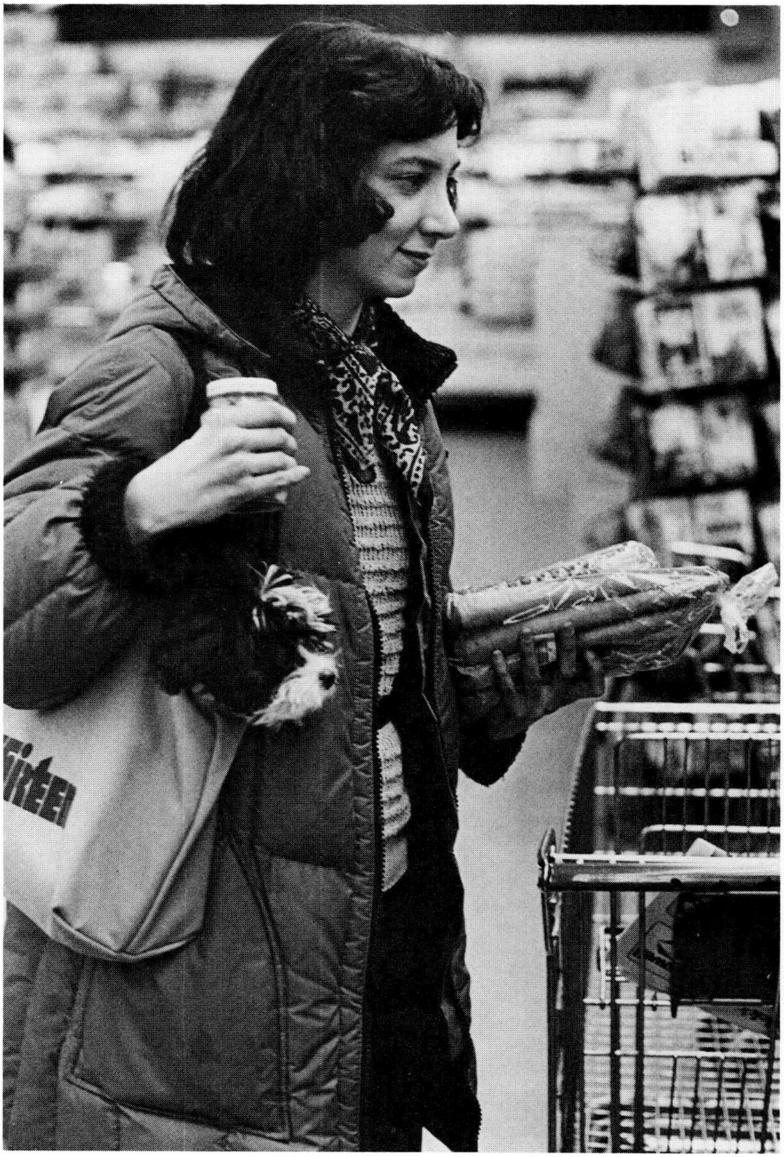

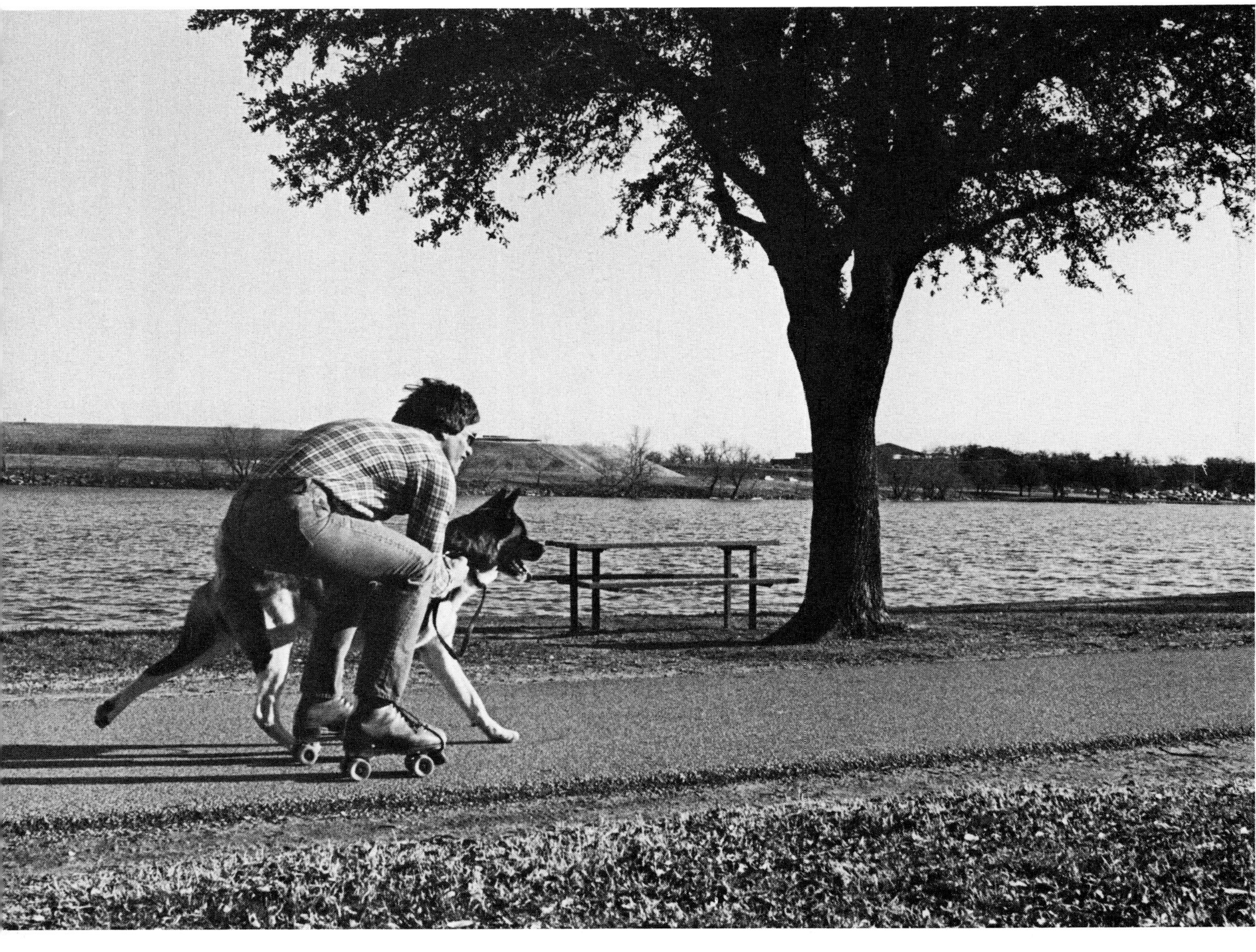

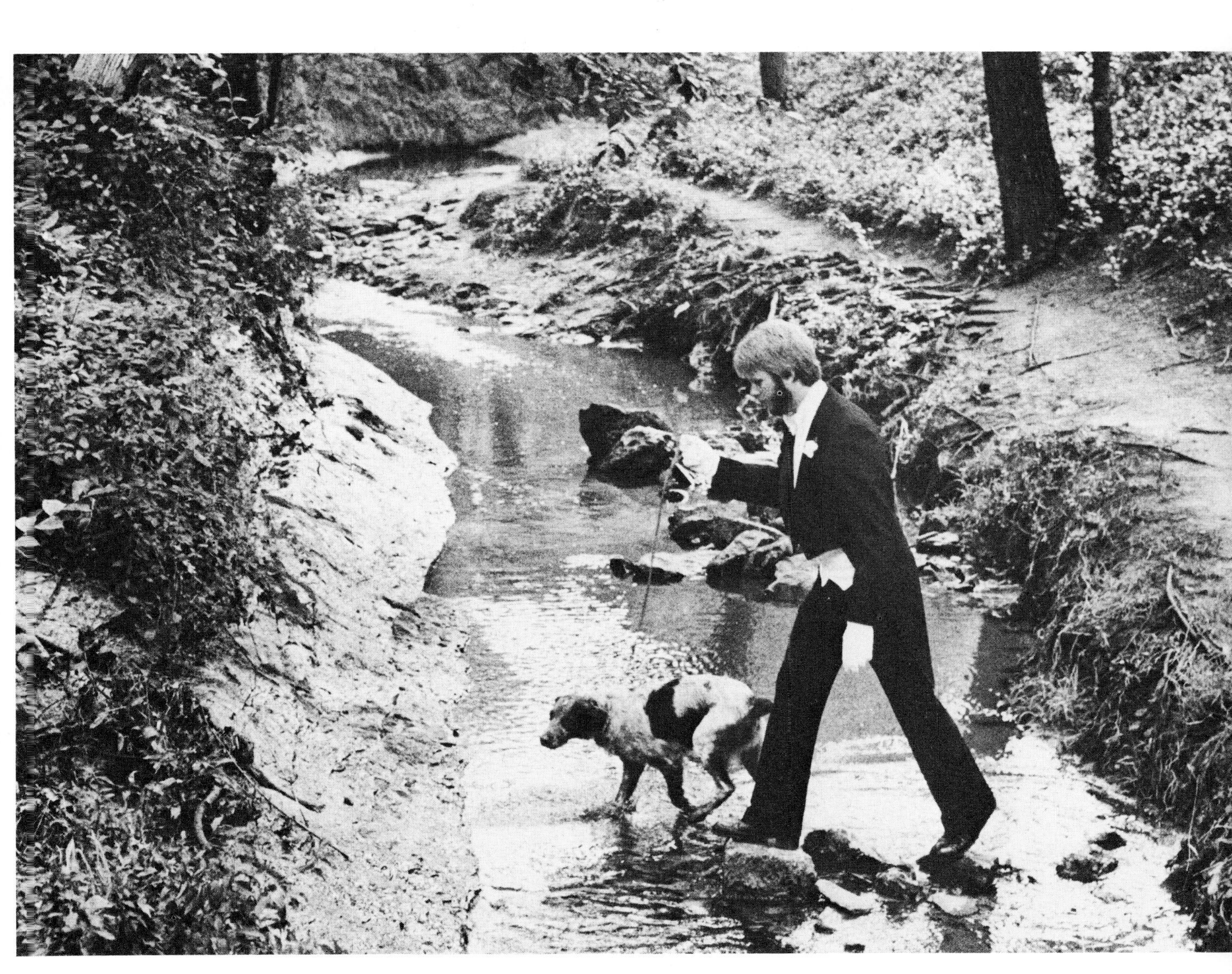

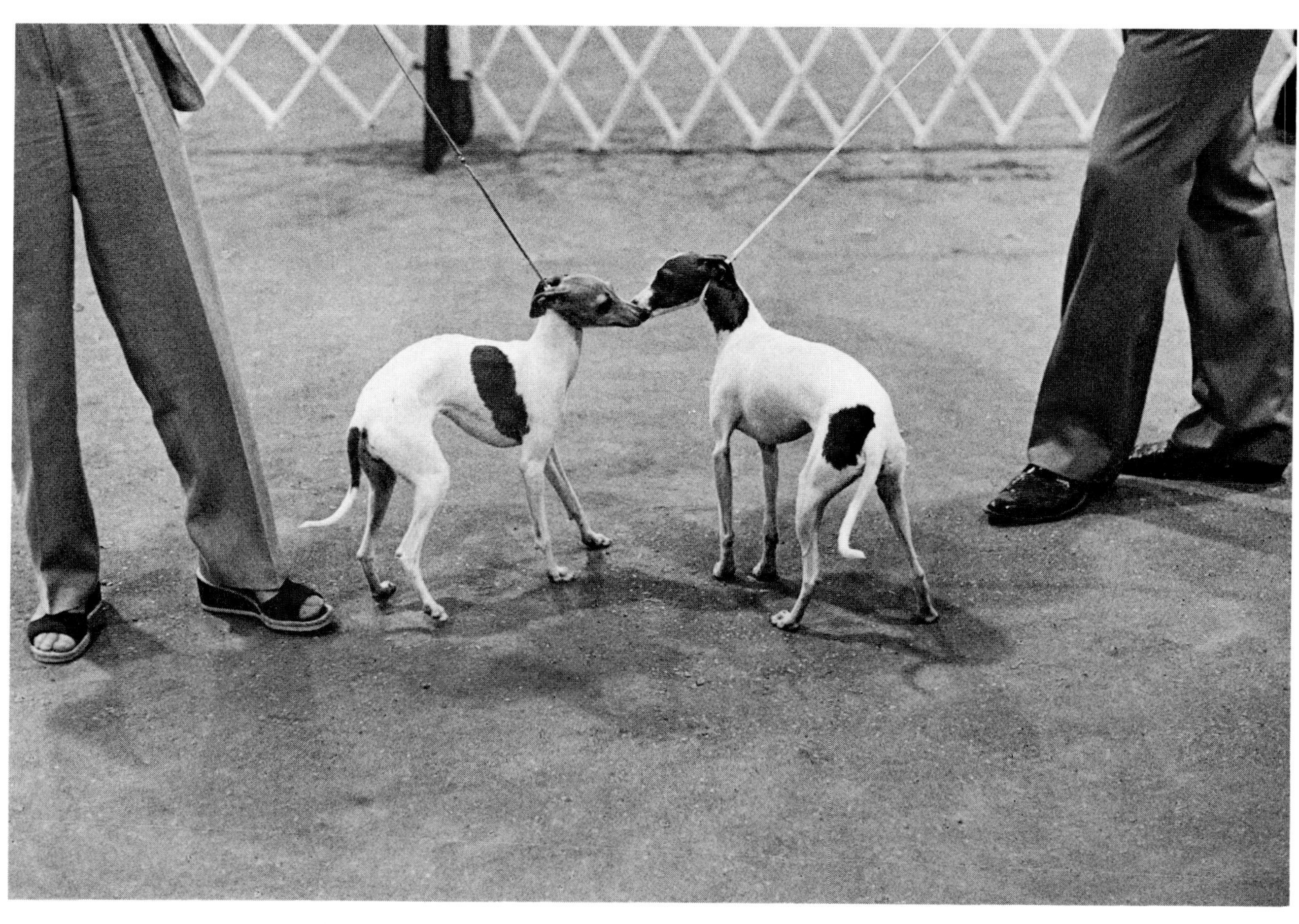

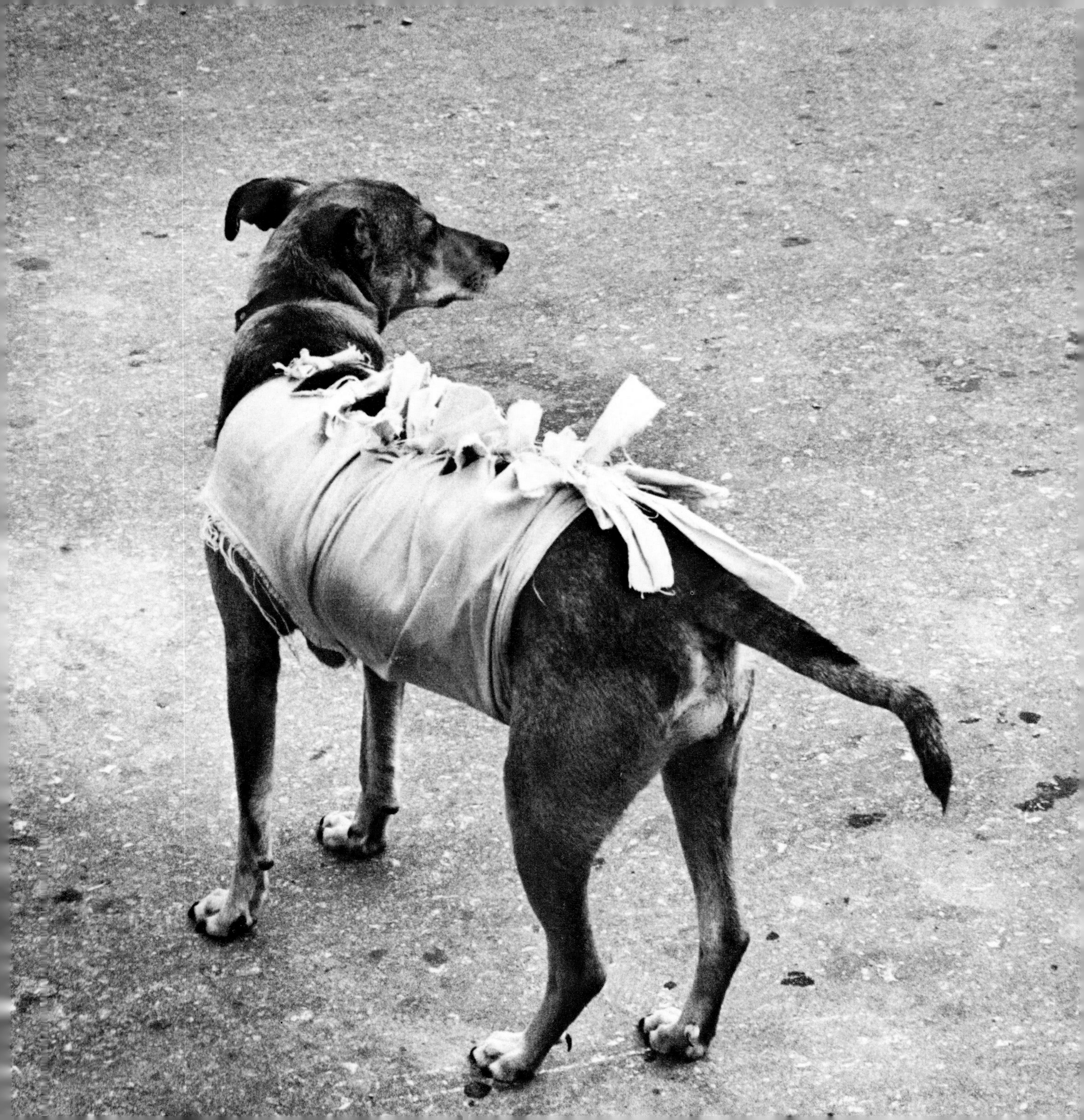

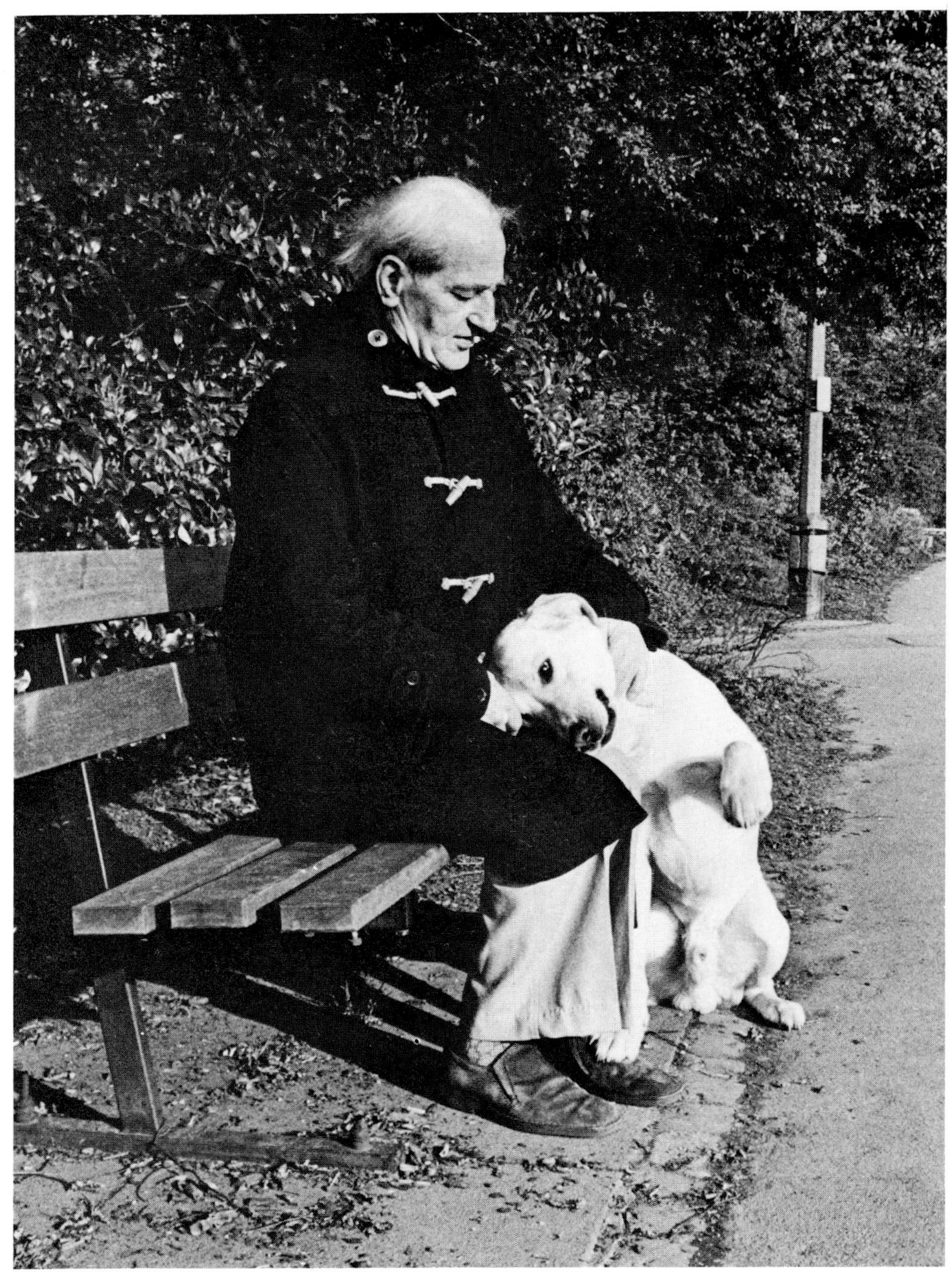

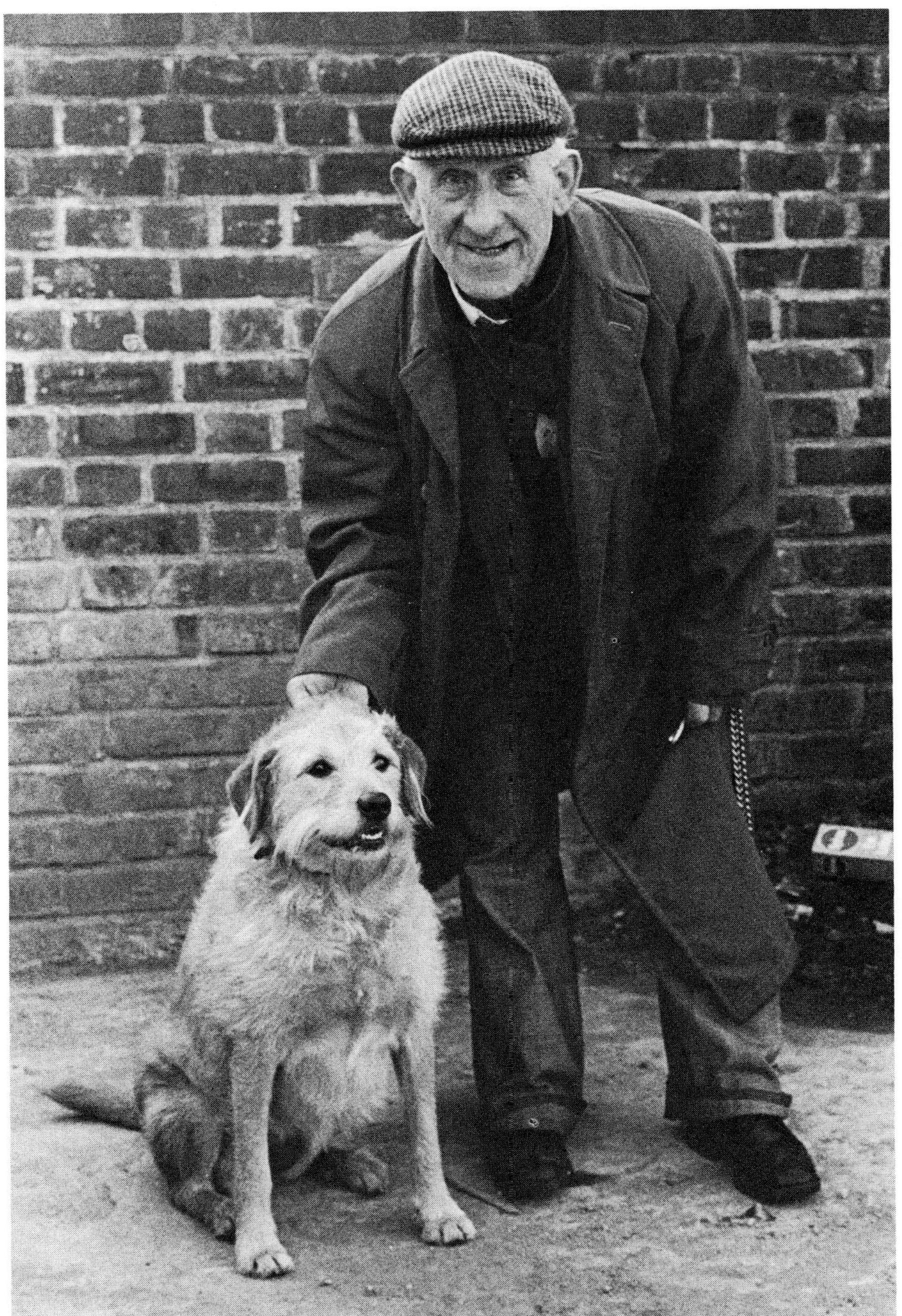

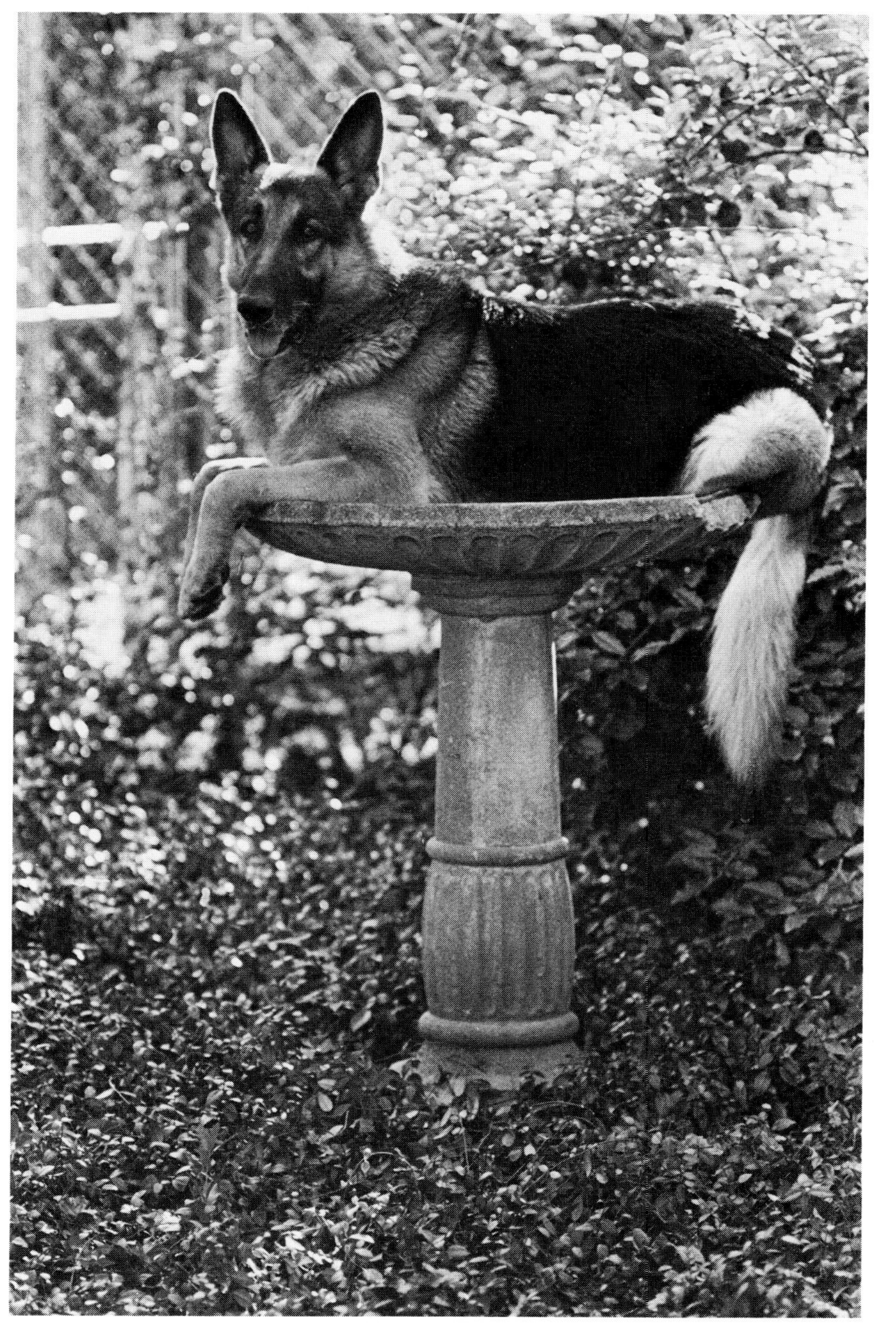

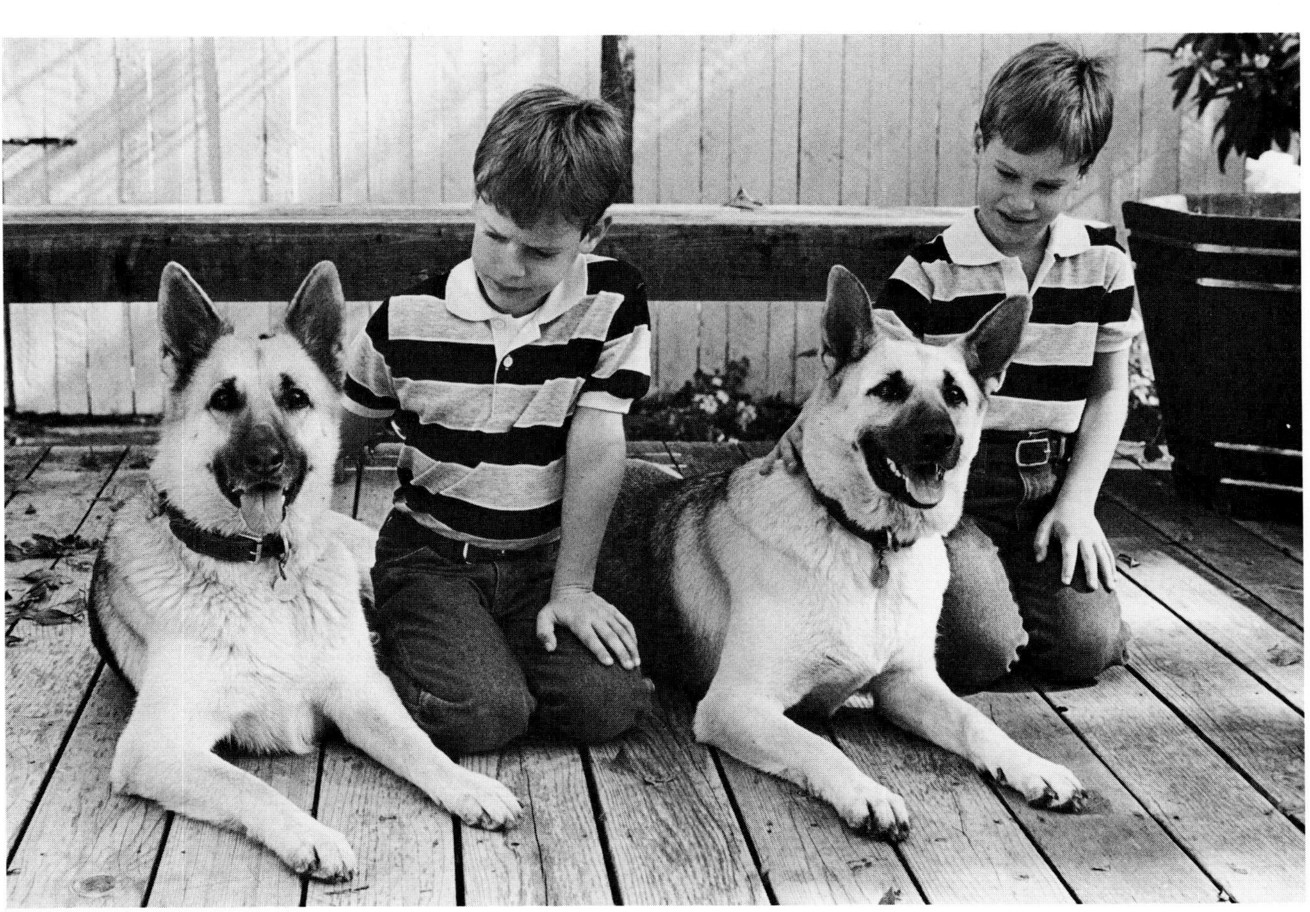

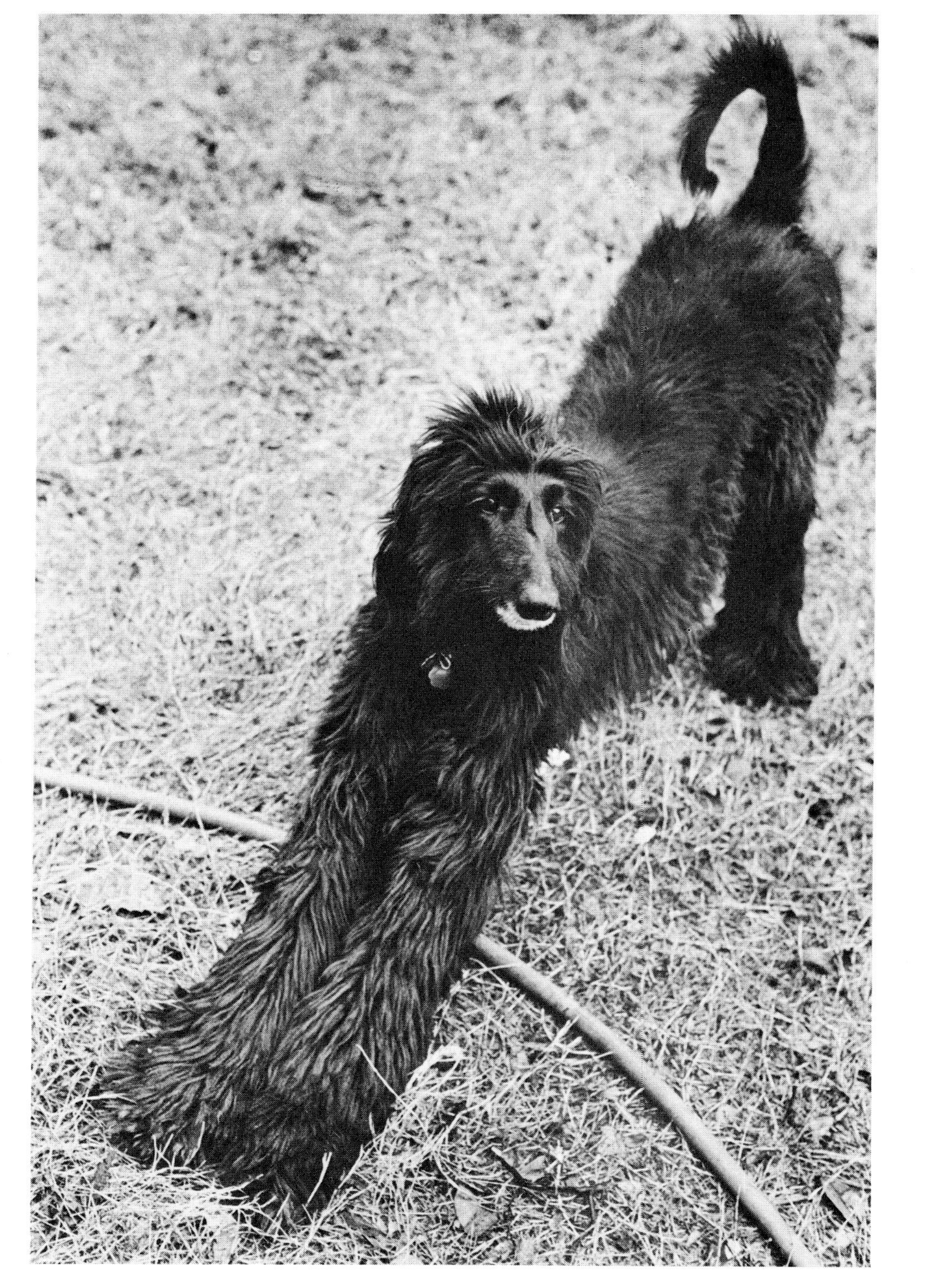

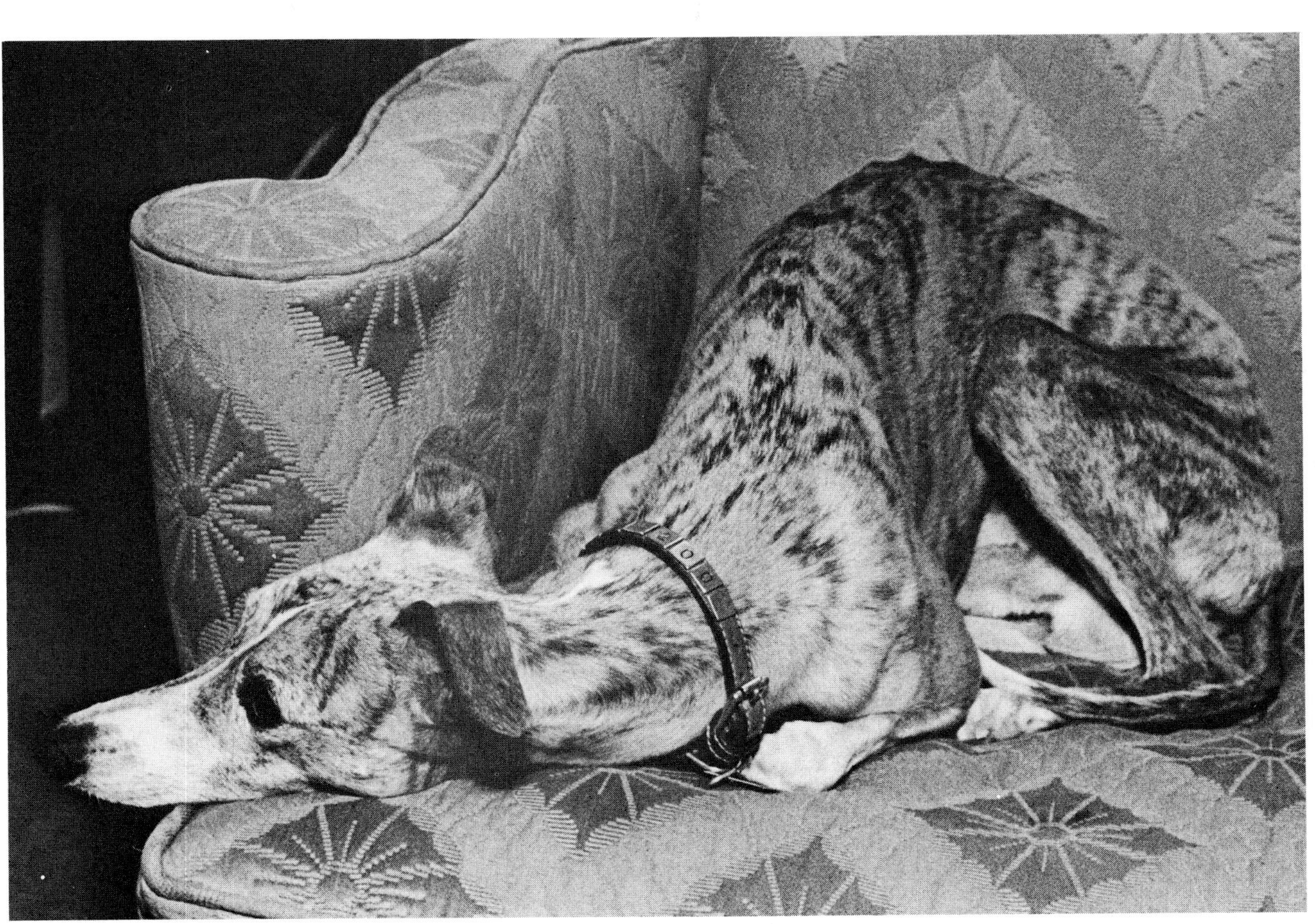

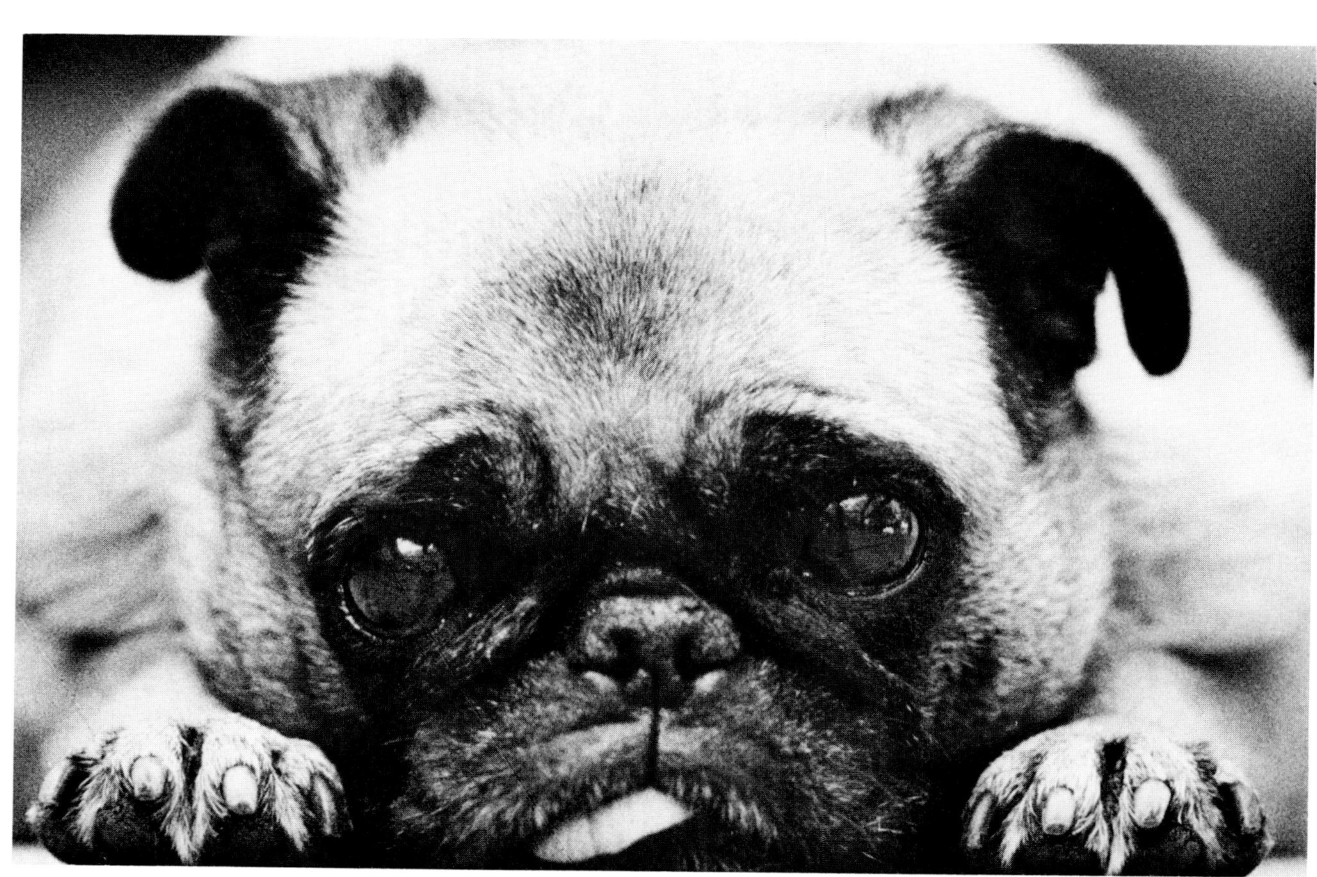

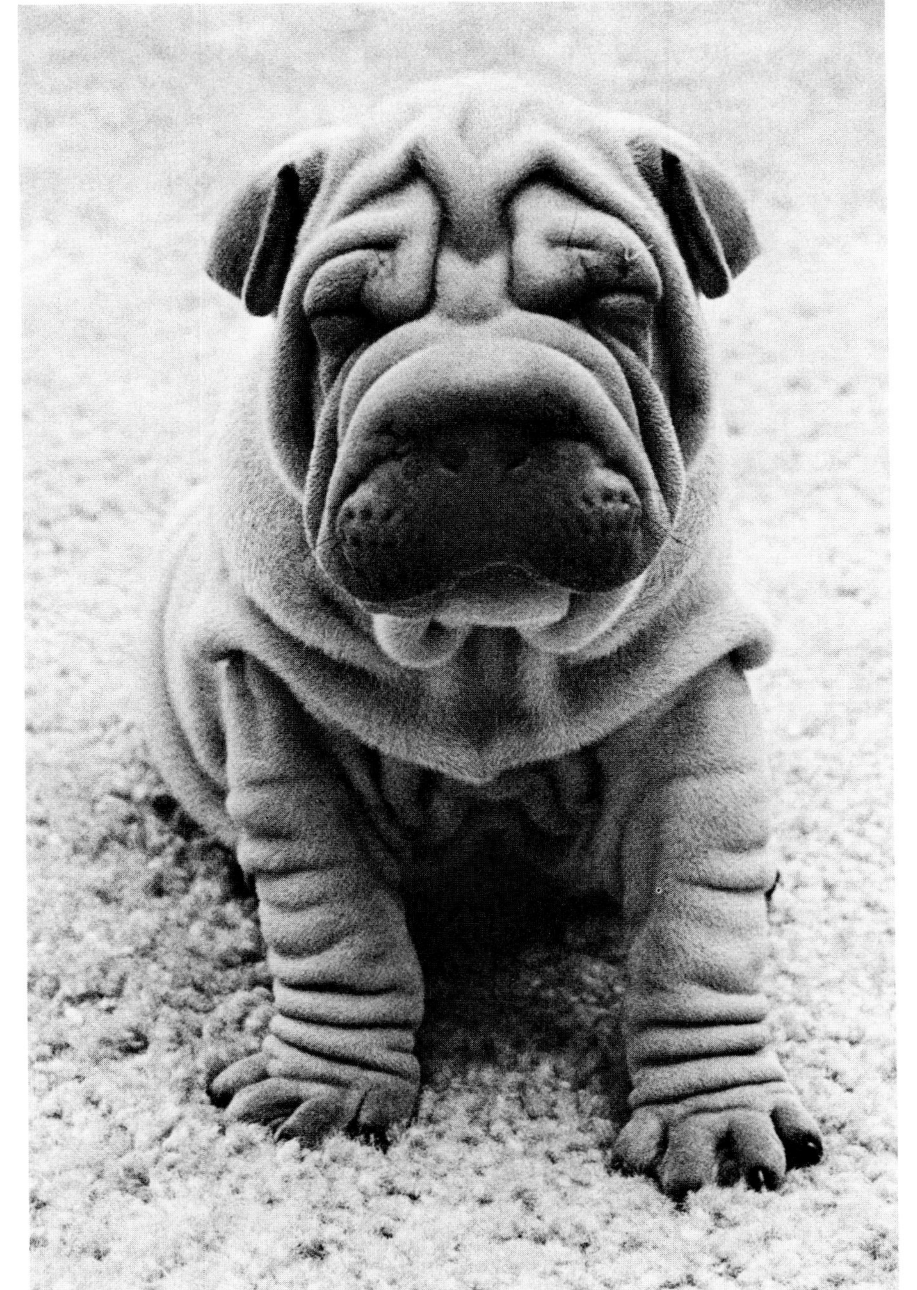

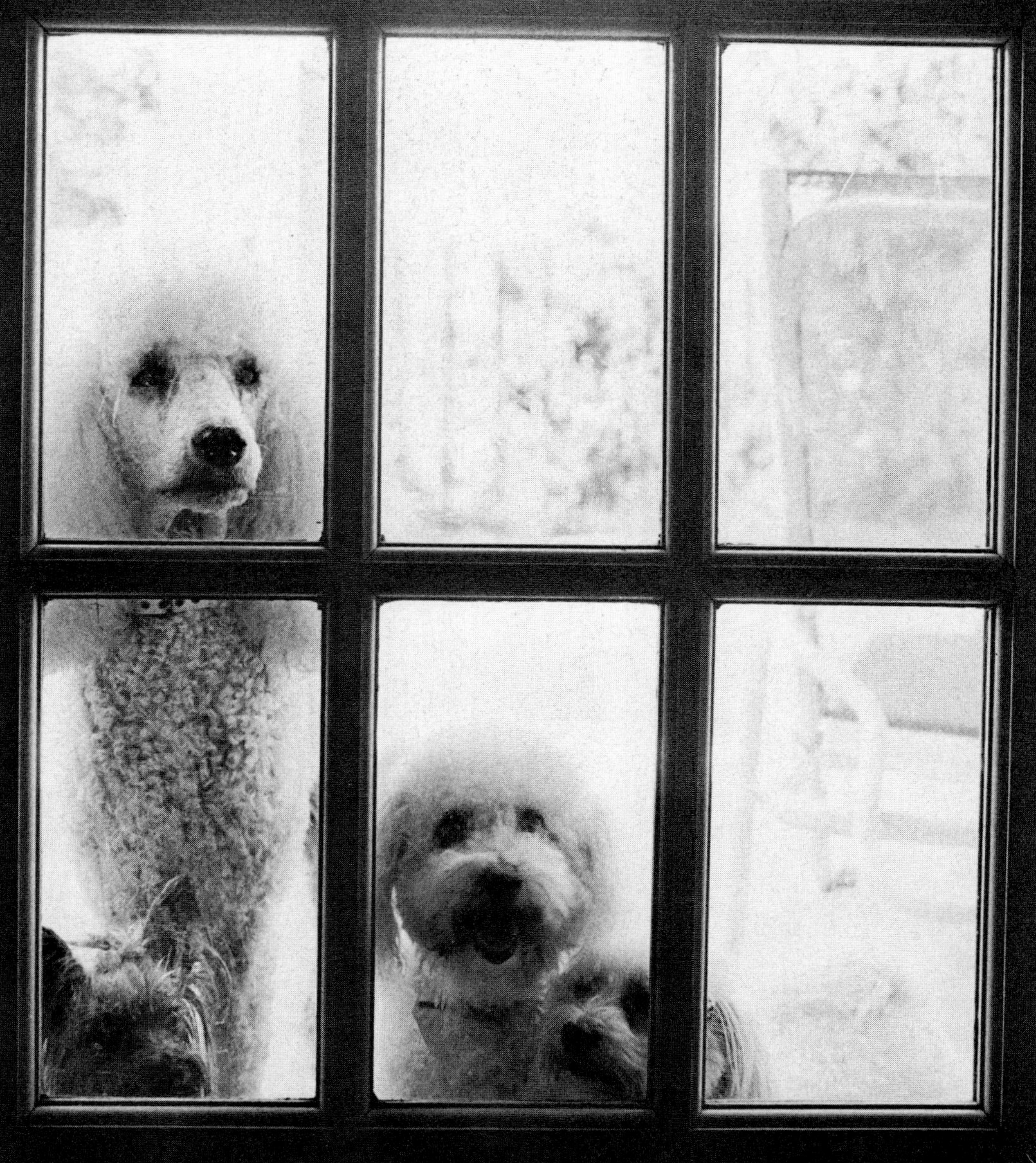

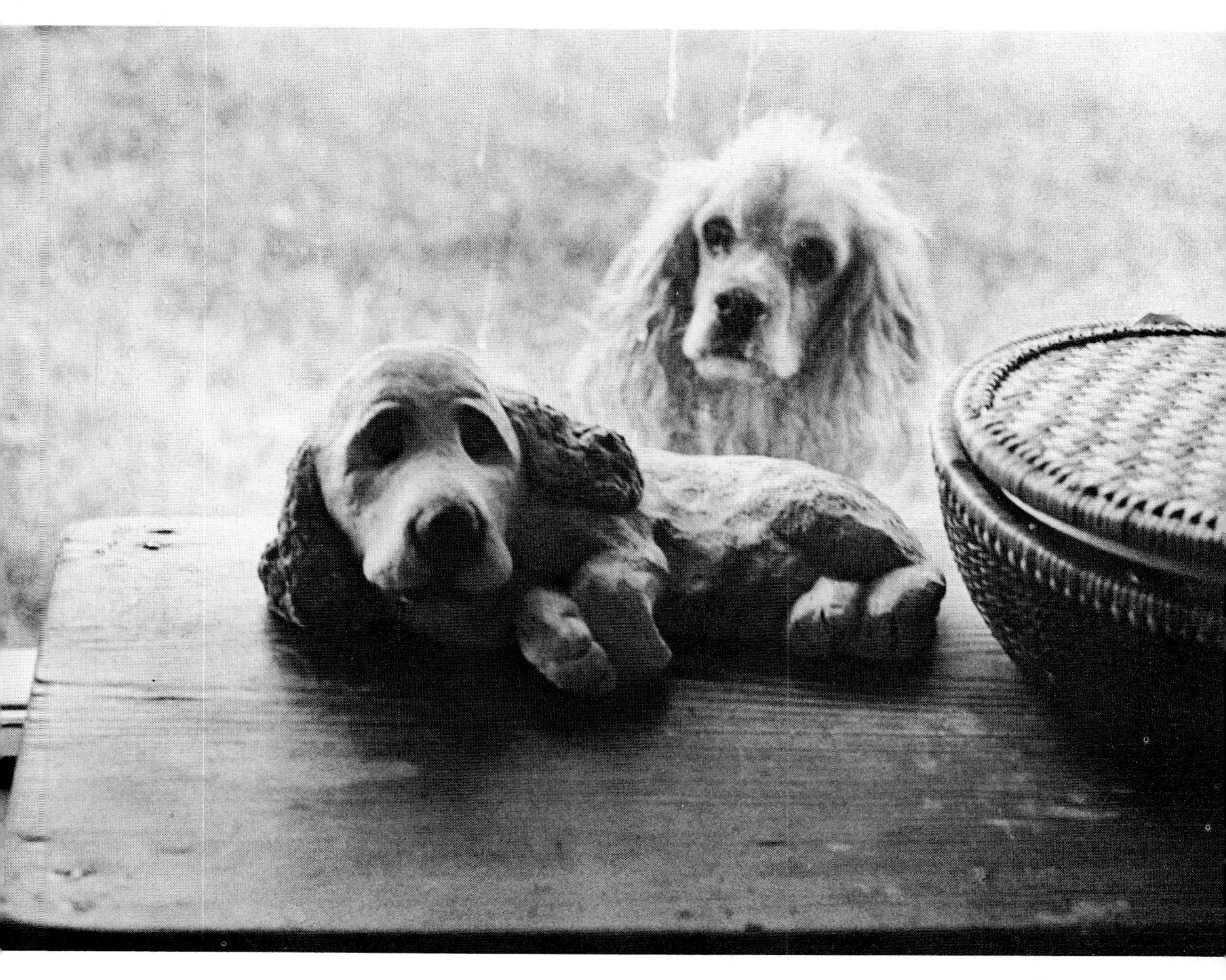

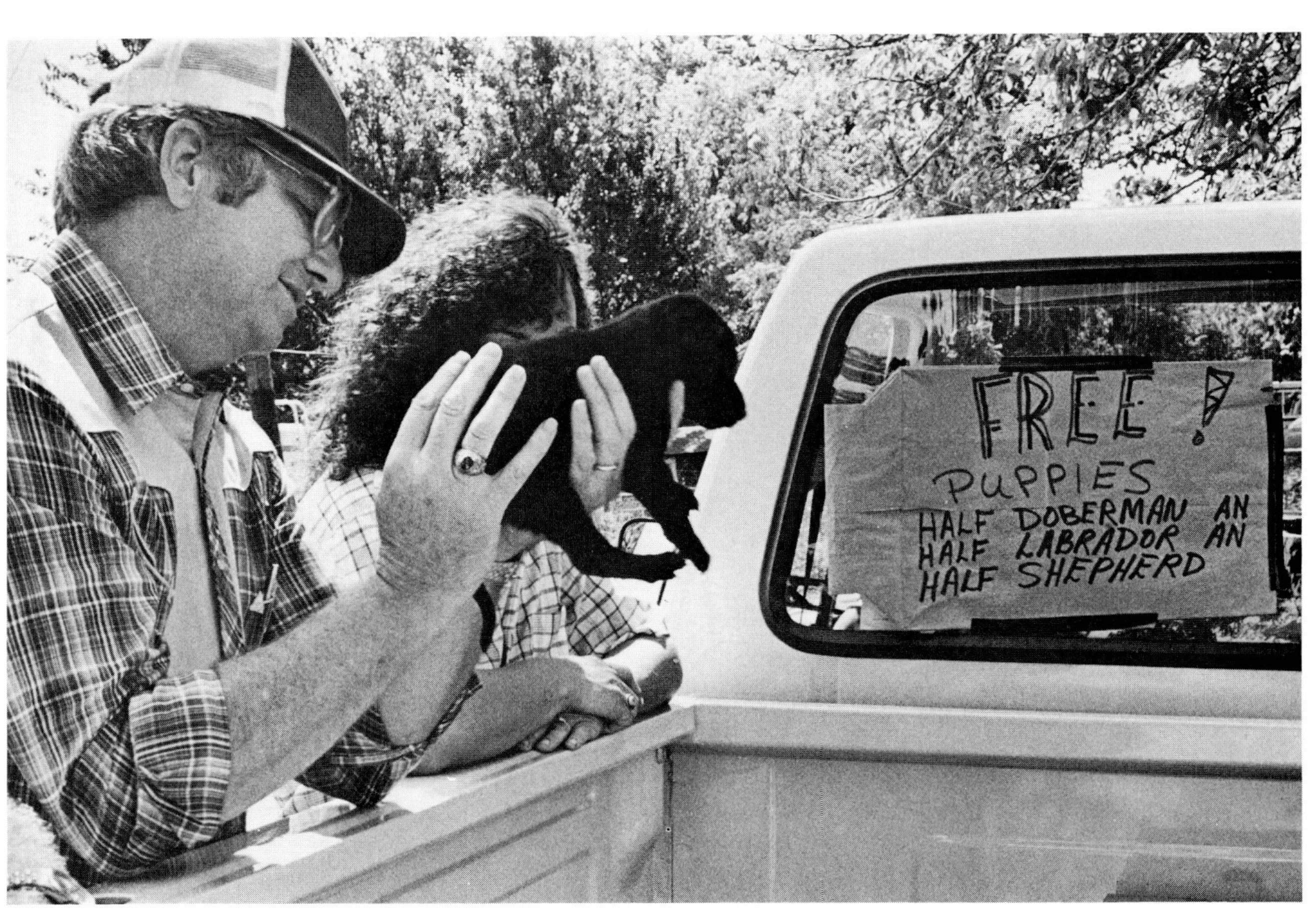
FREE!
PUPPIES
HALF DOBERMAN AN
HALF LABRADOR AN
HALF SHEPHERD

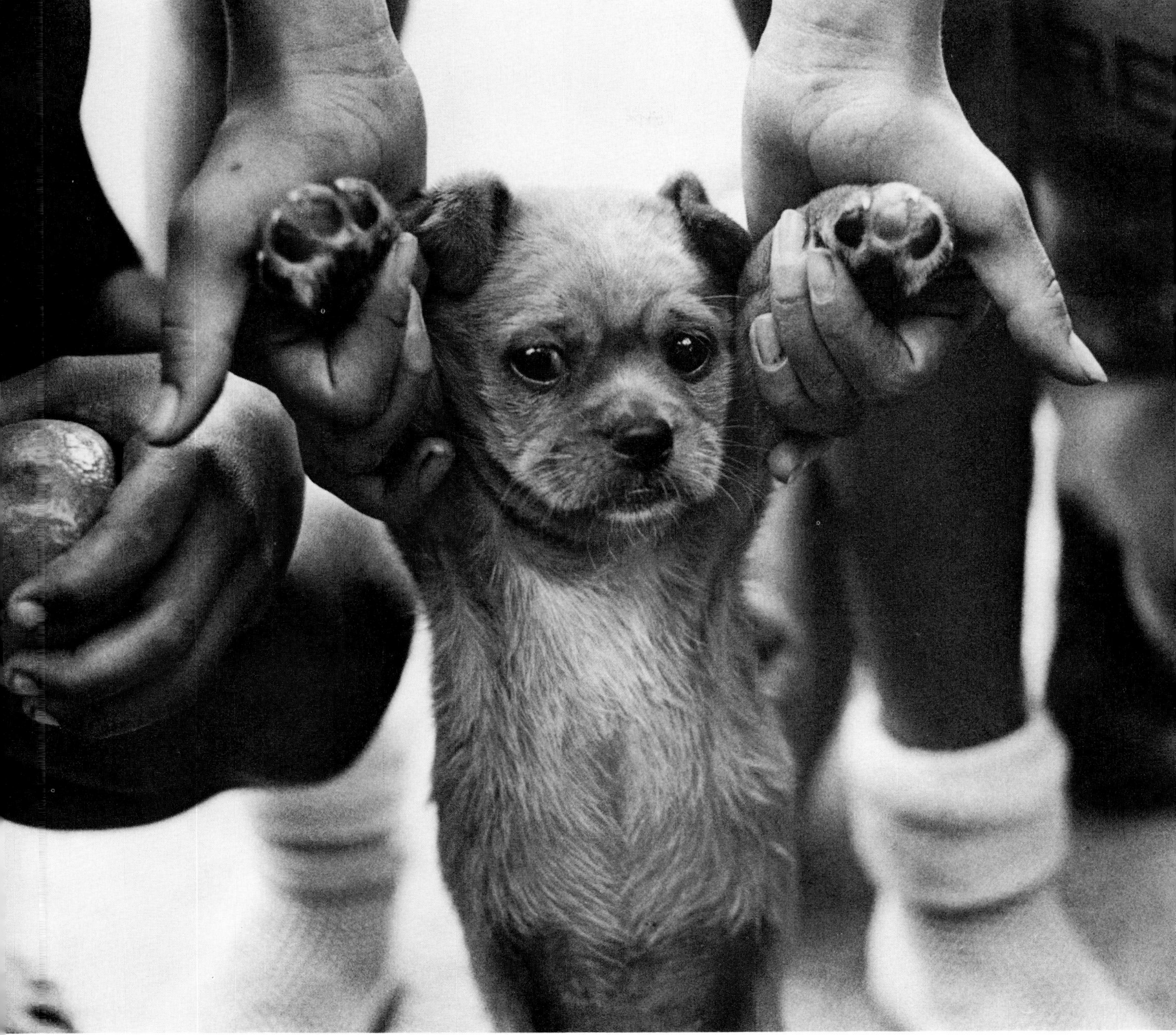

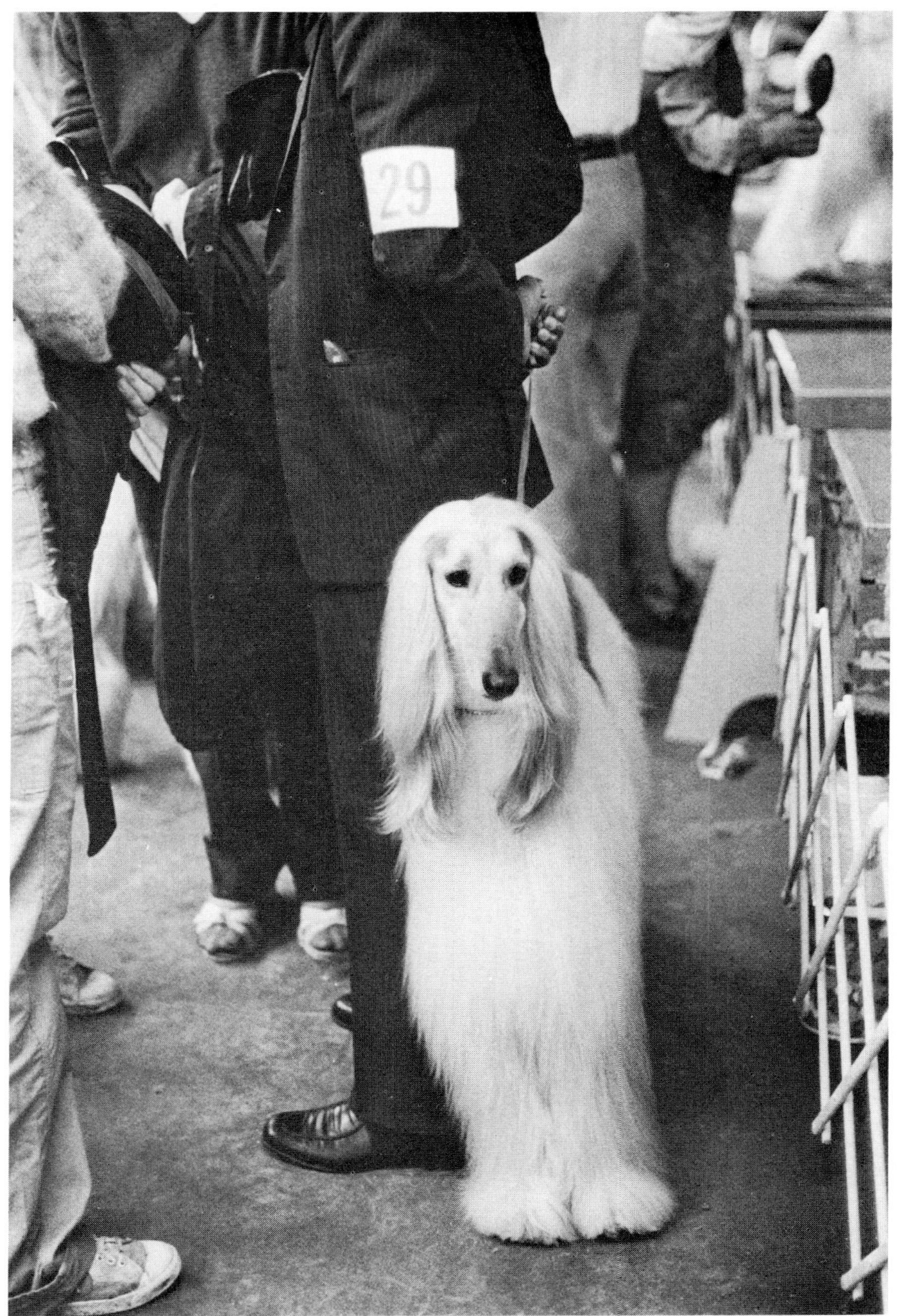
29

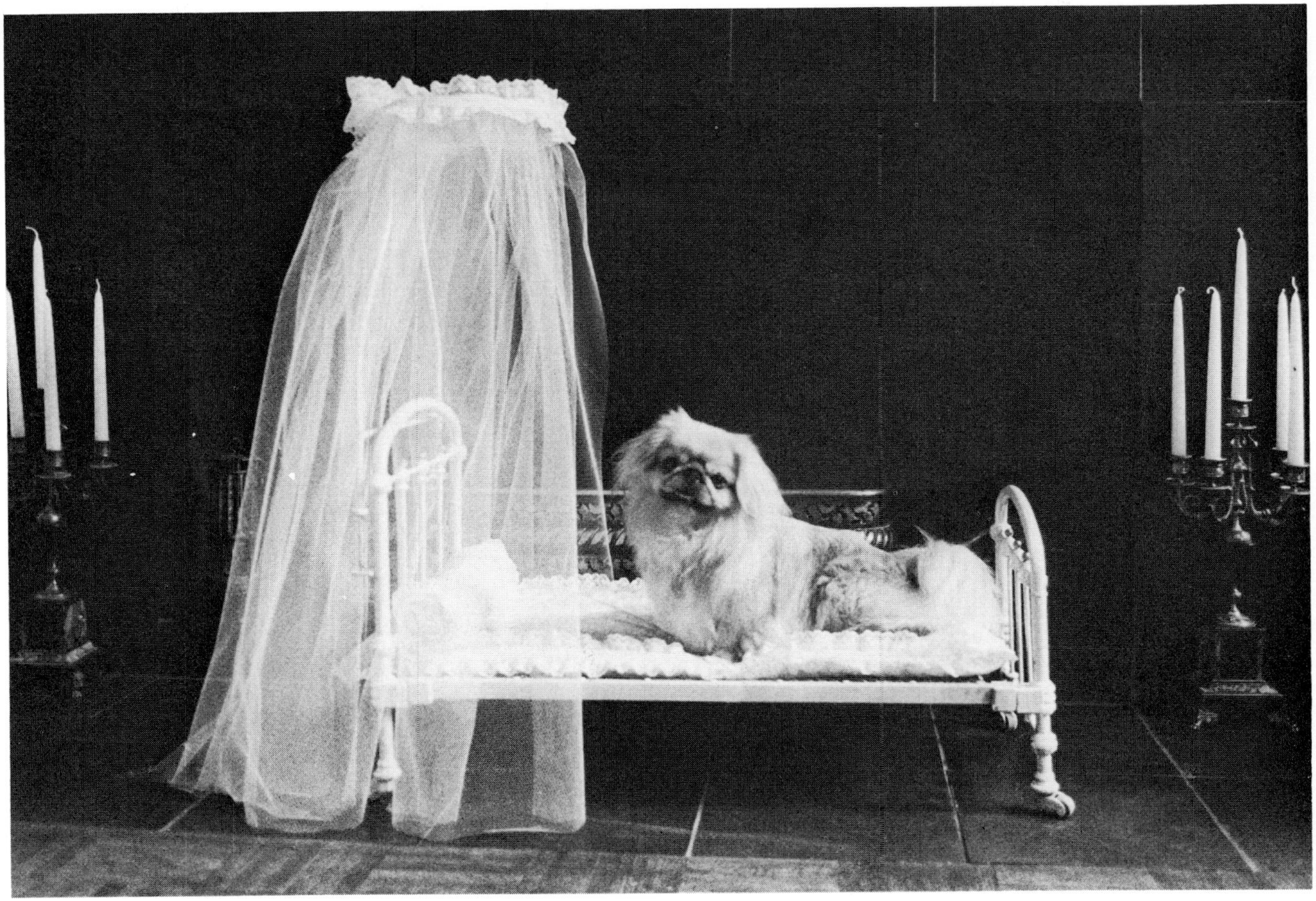

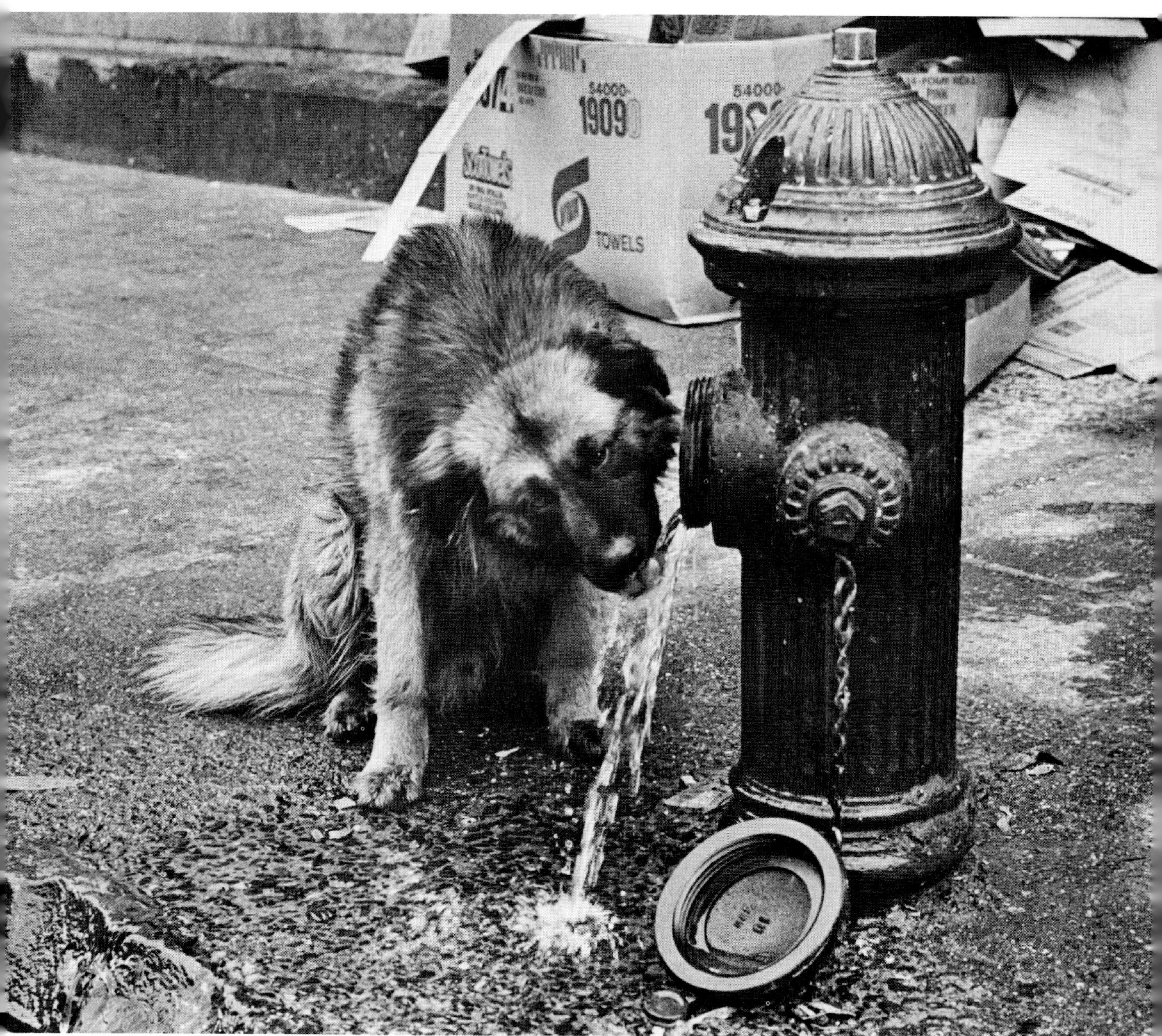

54000-
19090
TOWELS
54000-

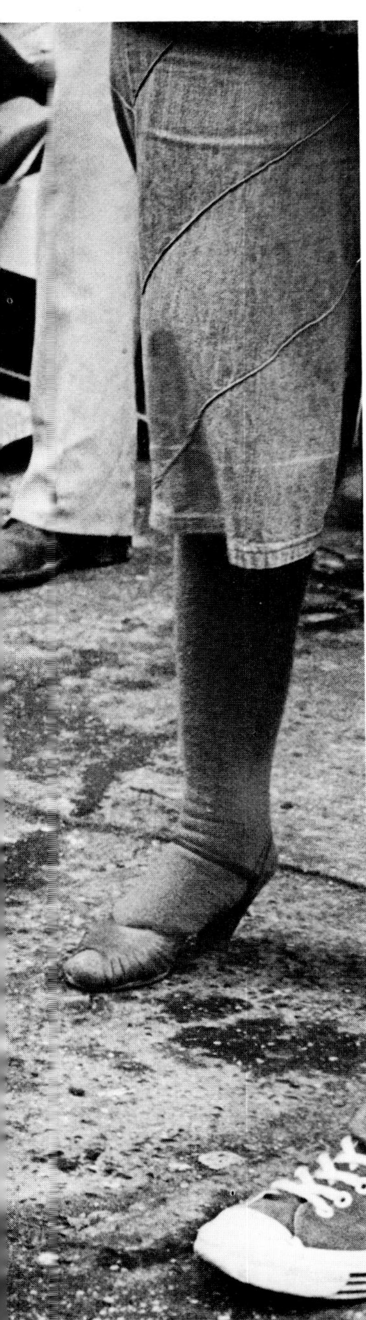

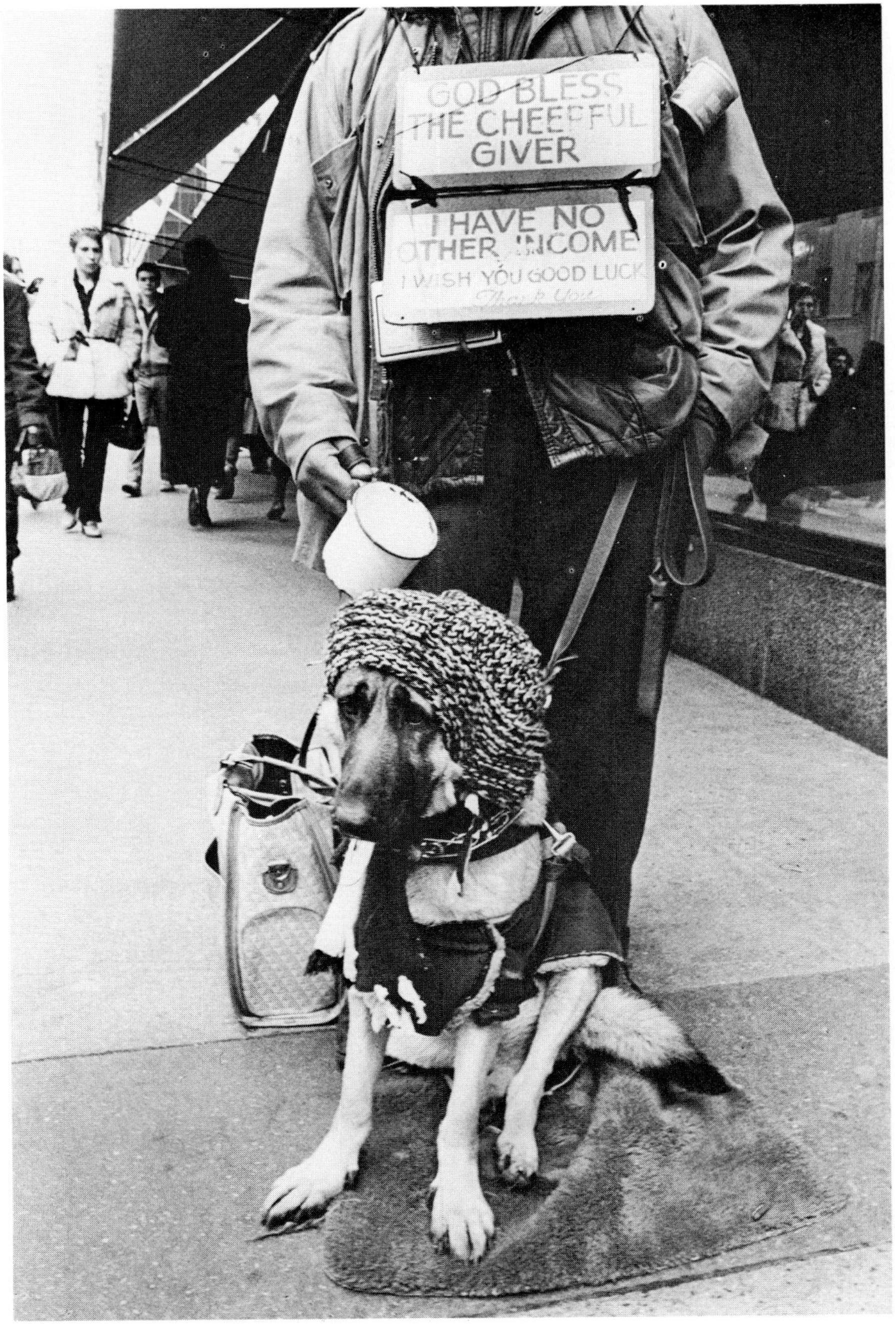

GOD BLESS
THE CHEEPFUL
GIVER
I HAVE NO
OTHER INCOME
I WISH YOU GOOD LUCK

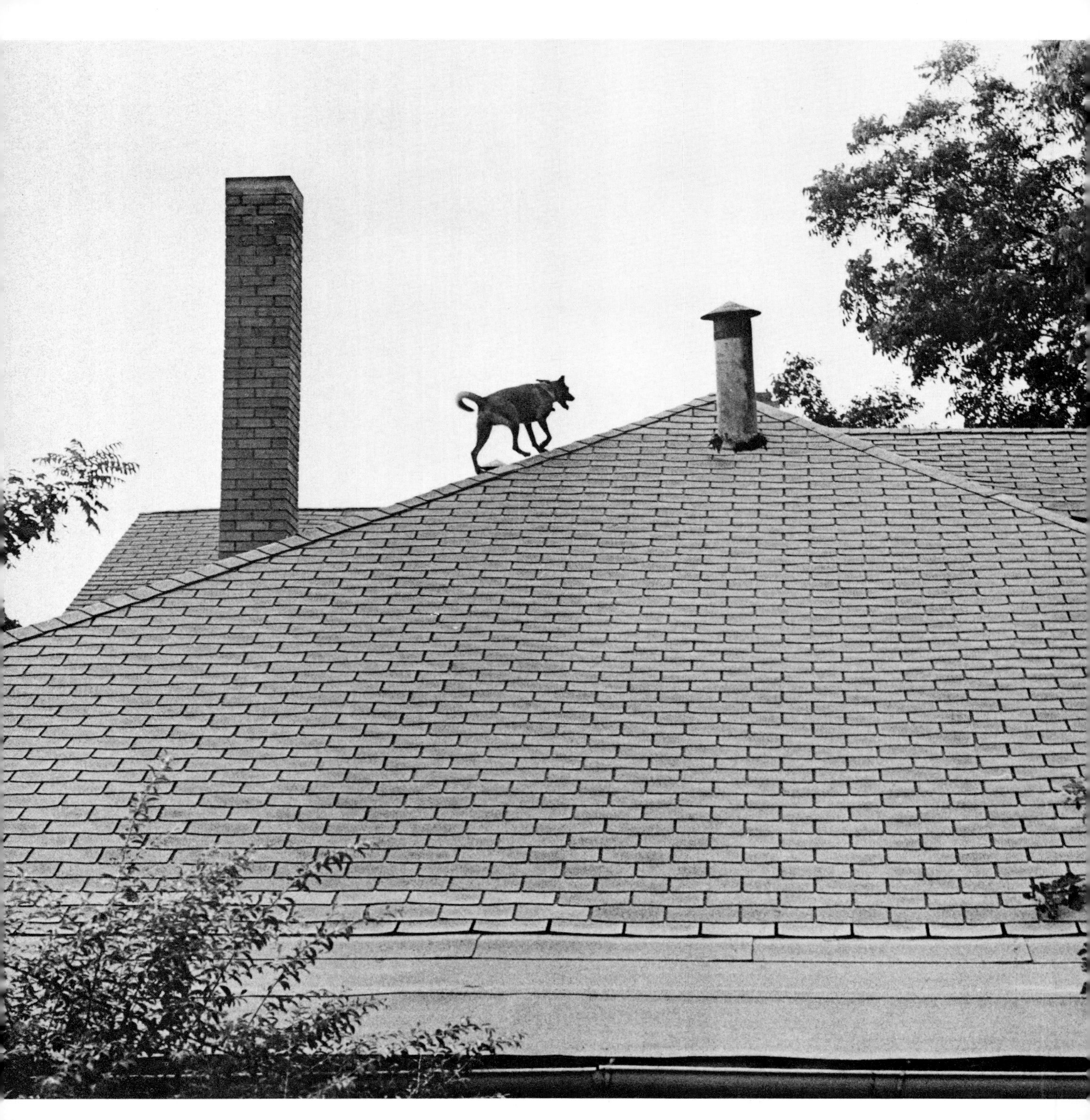

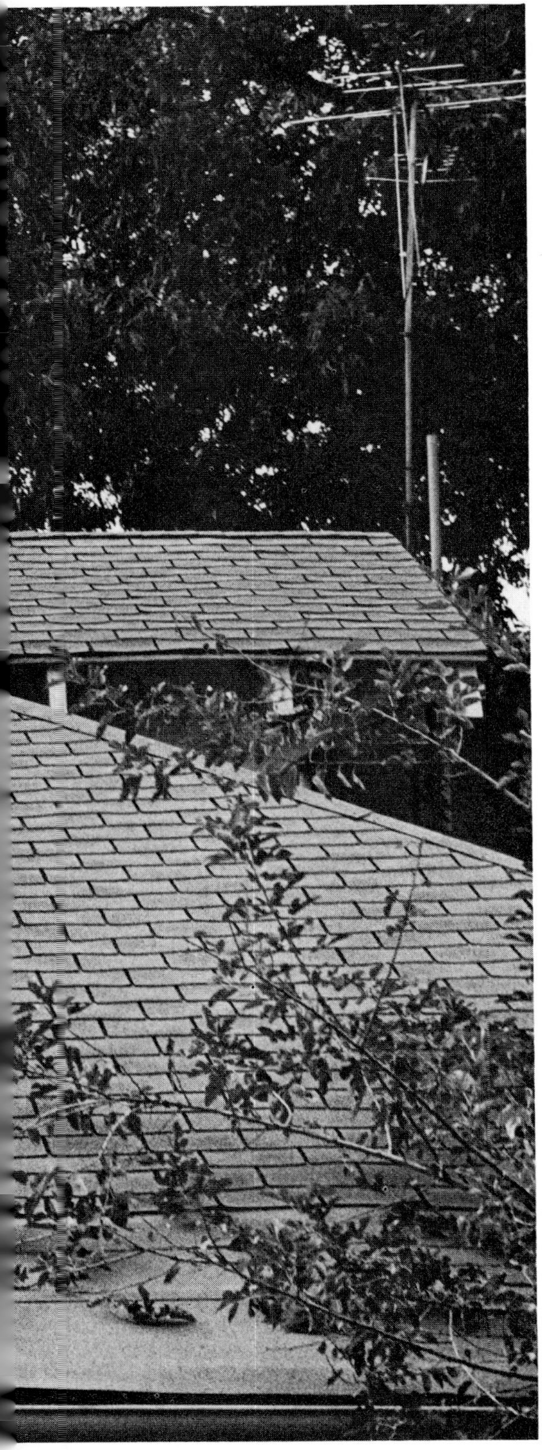

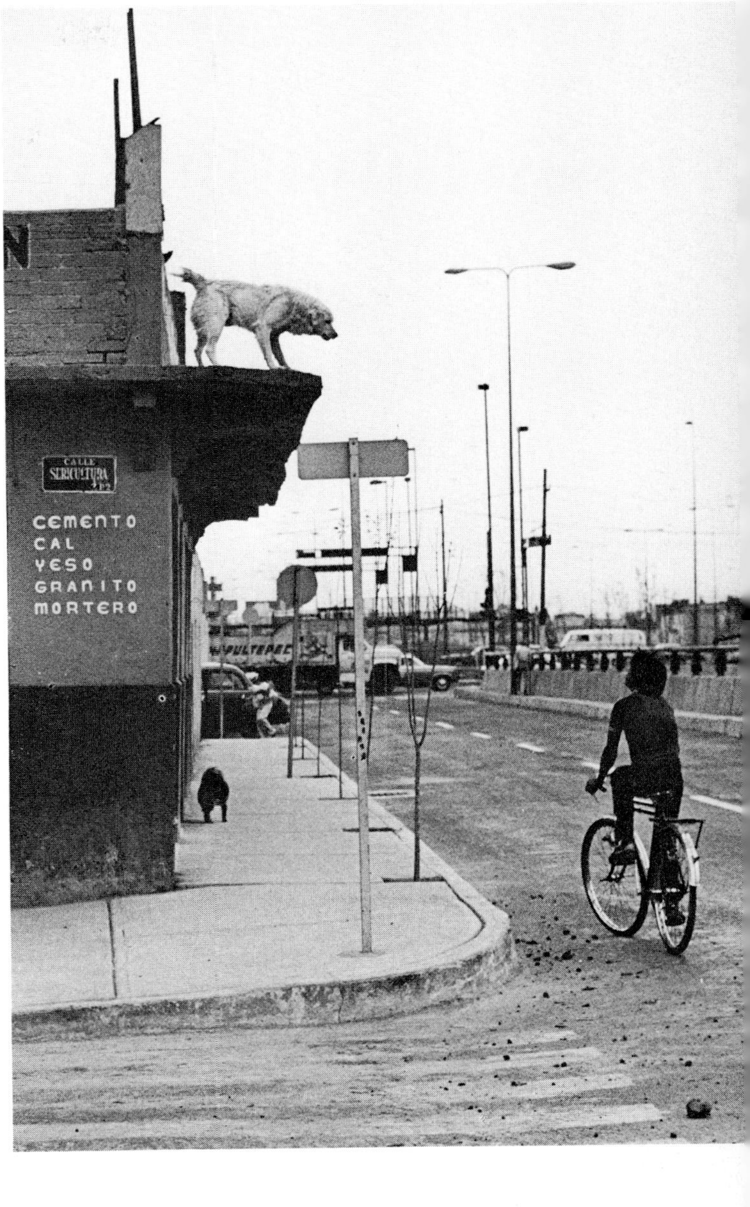

CALLE
SERICULTURA
CEMENTO
CAL
YESO
GRANITO
MORTERO

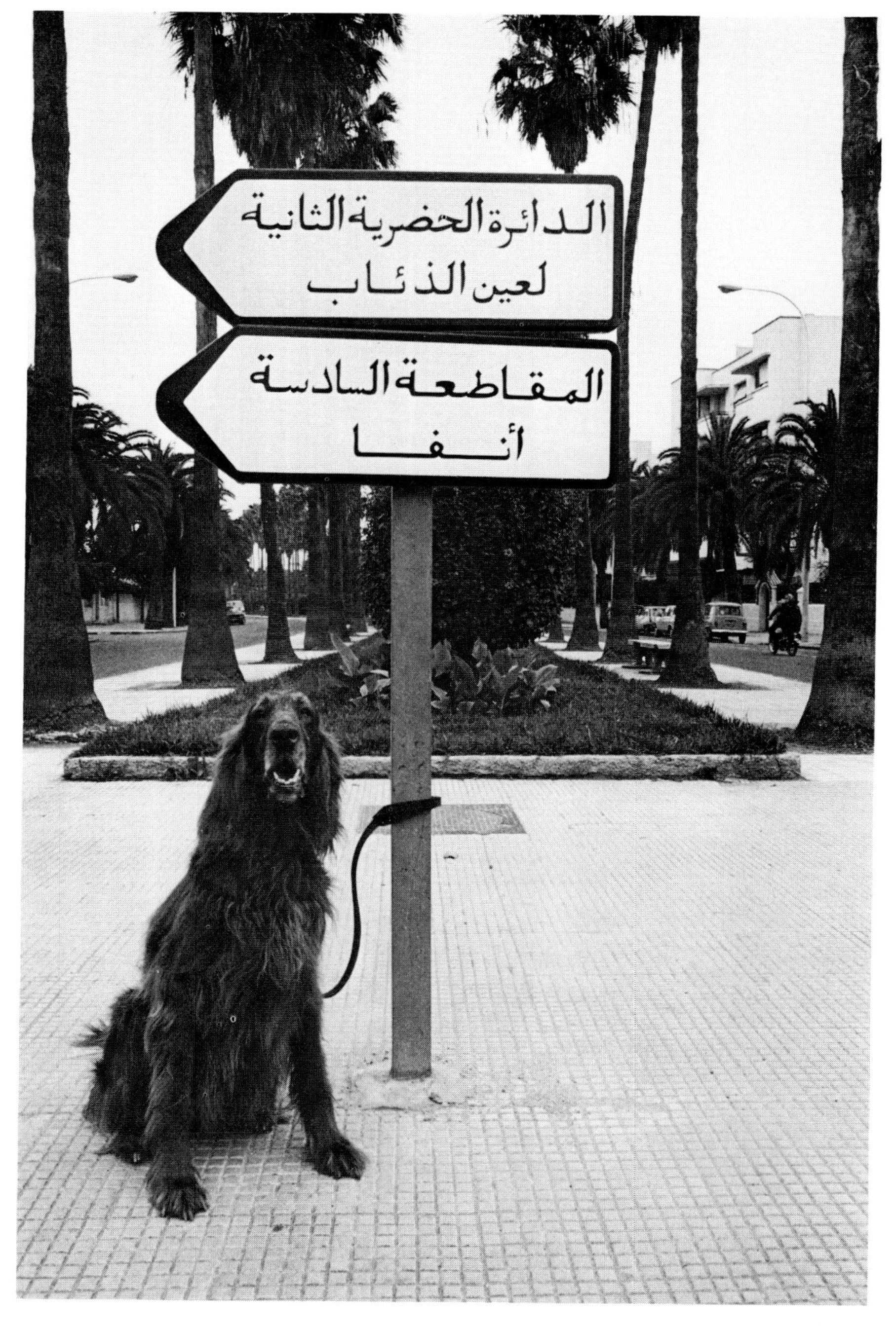

الدائرة الحضرية الثانية
لعين الذئاب
المقاطعة السادسة
أنفا

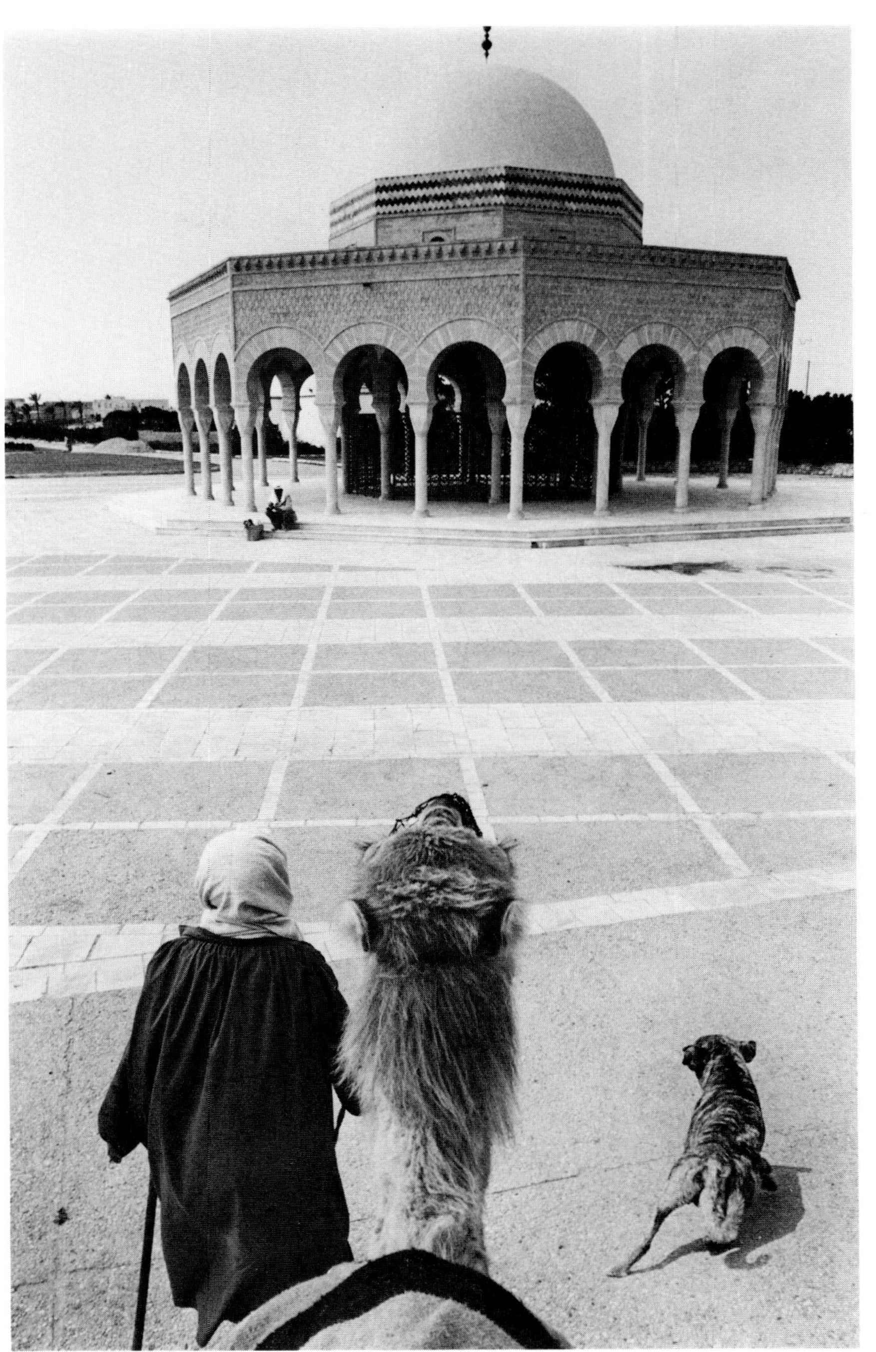

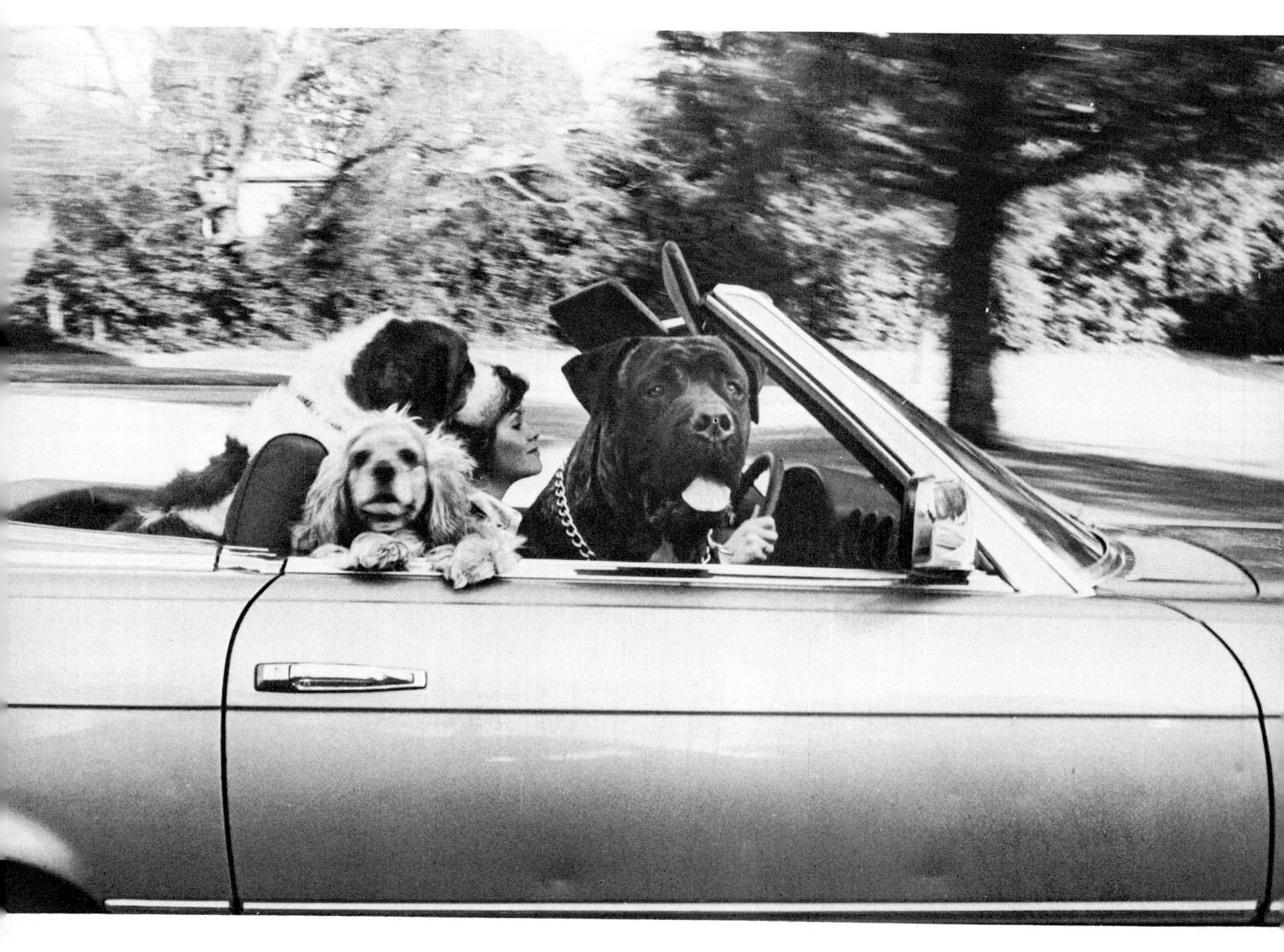

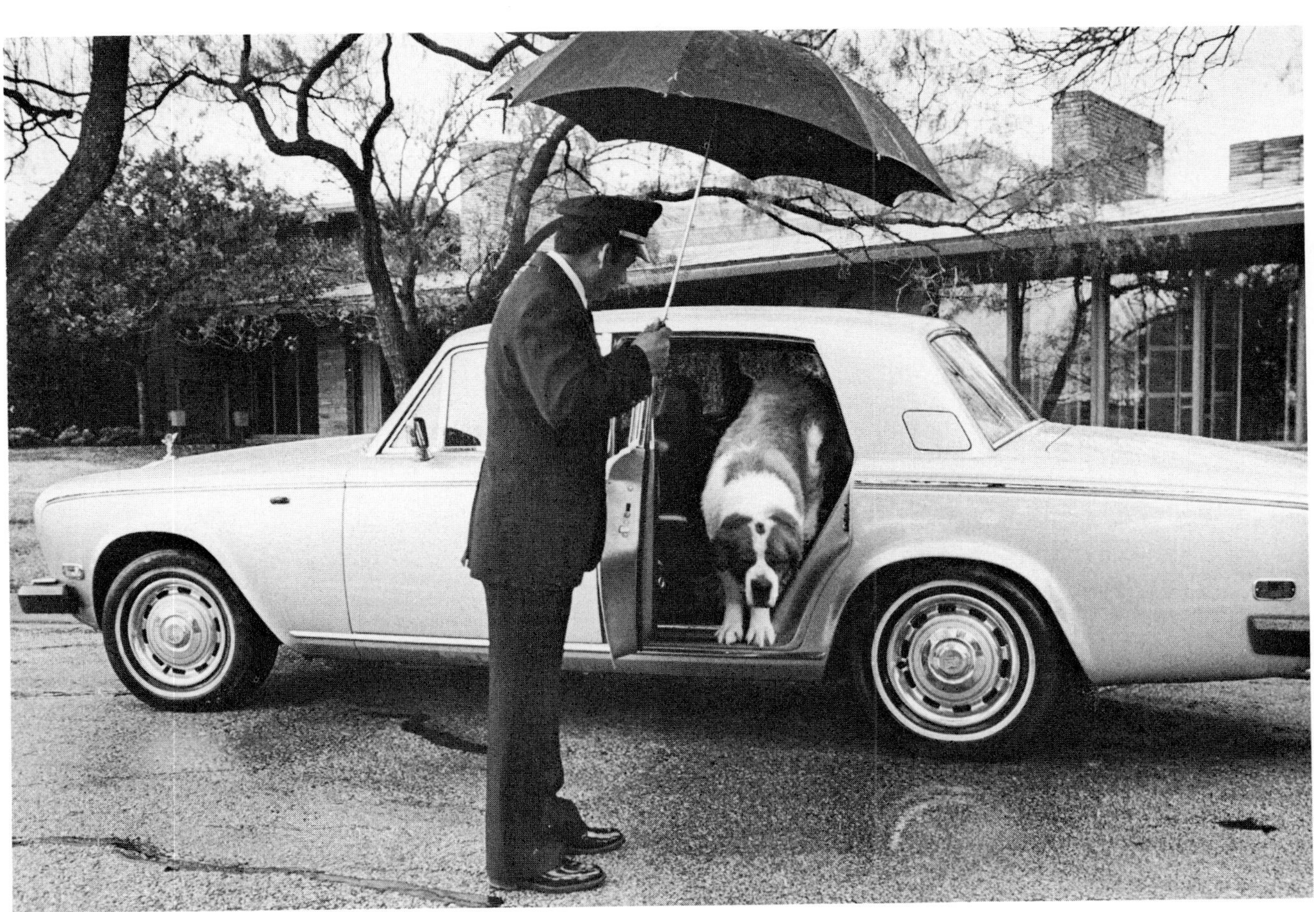

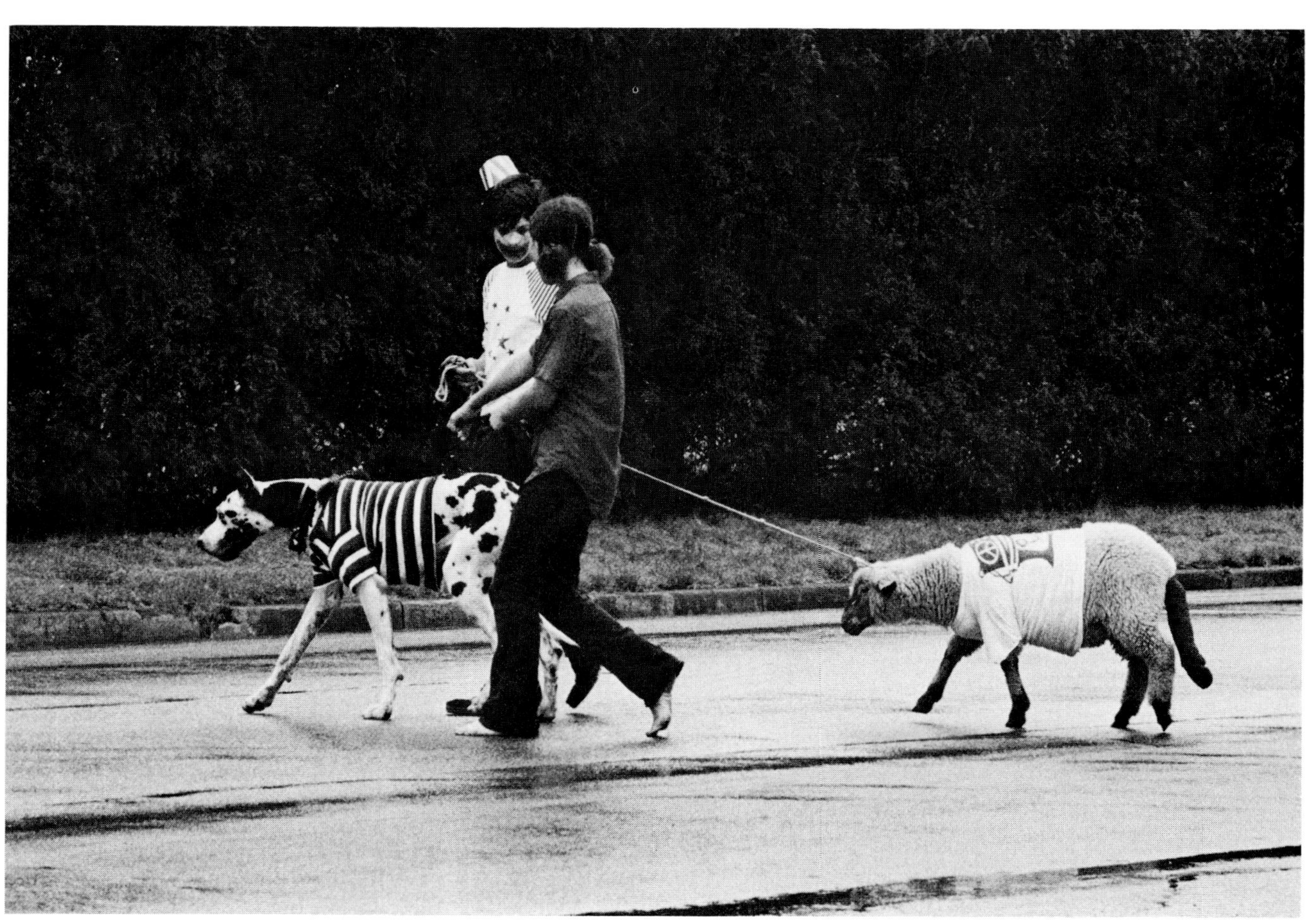

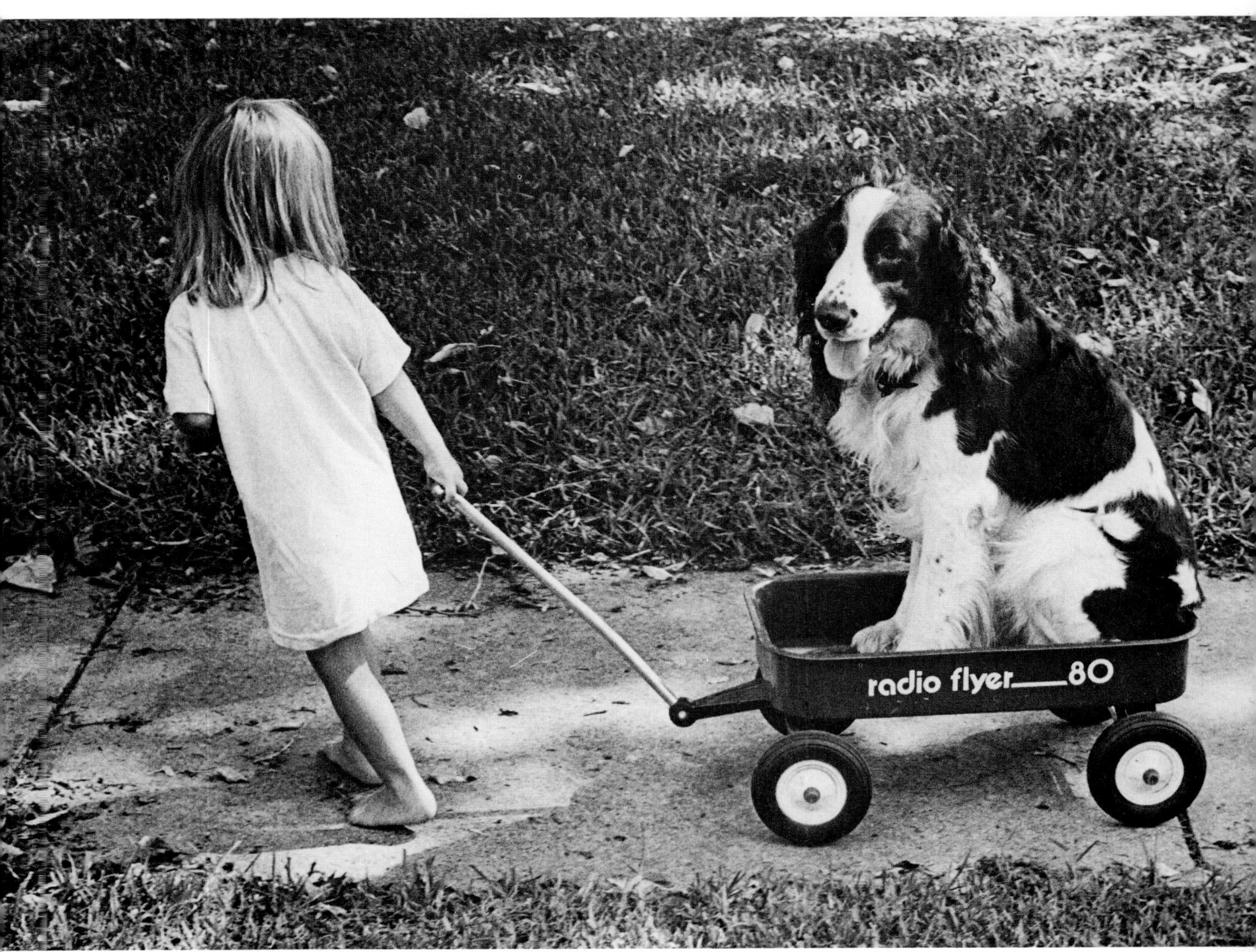
radio flyer 80

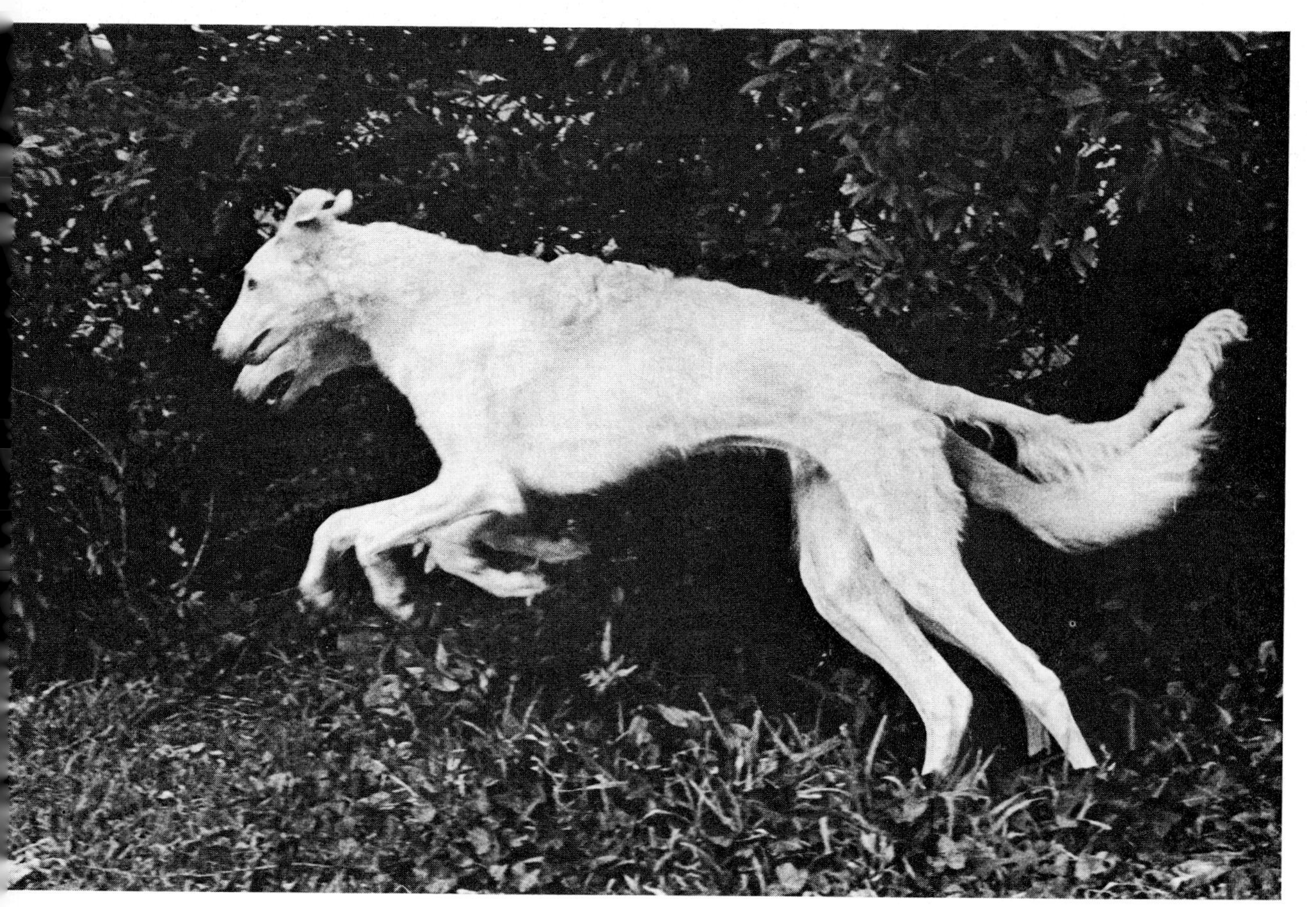

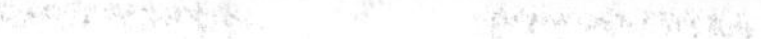

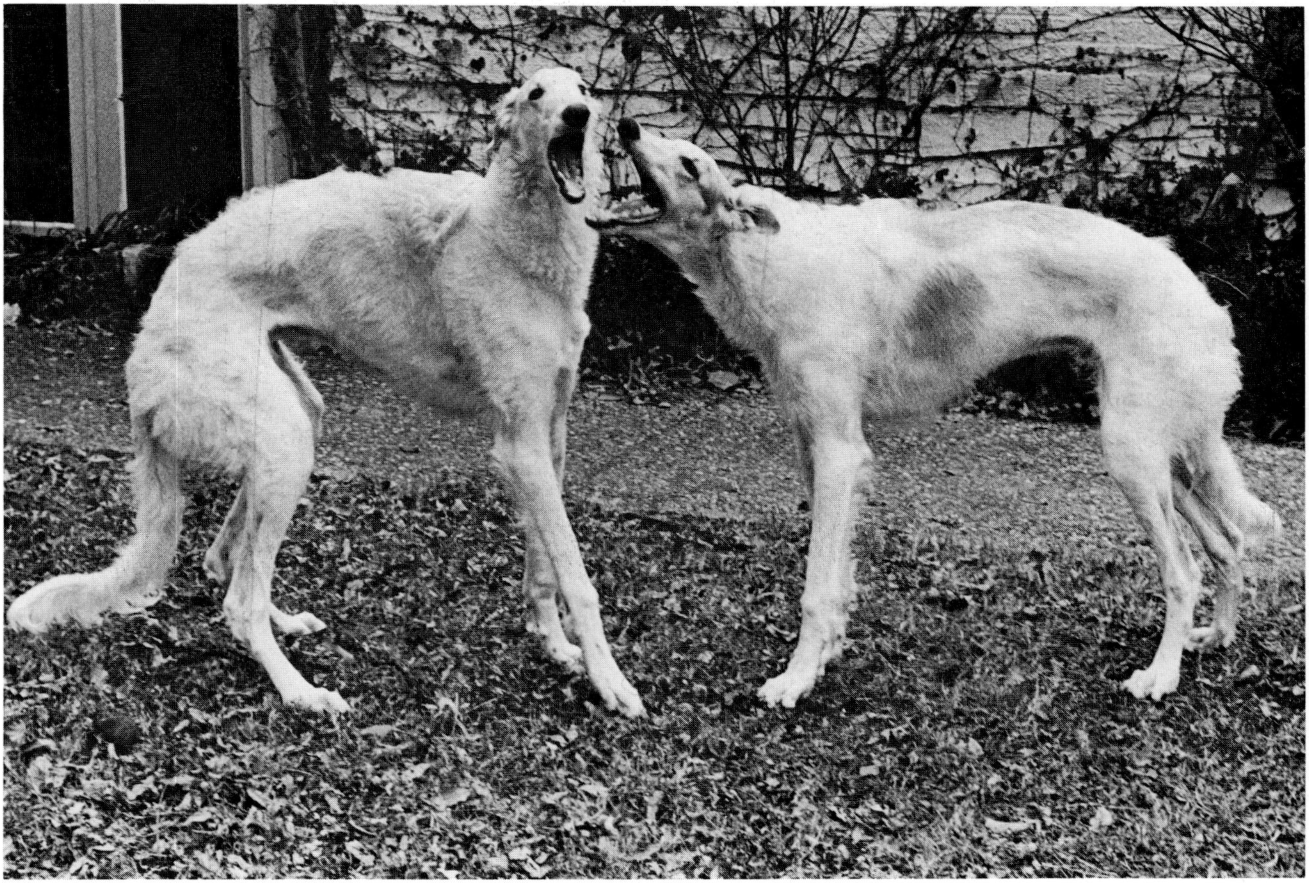

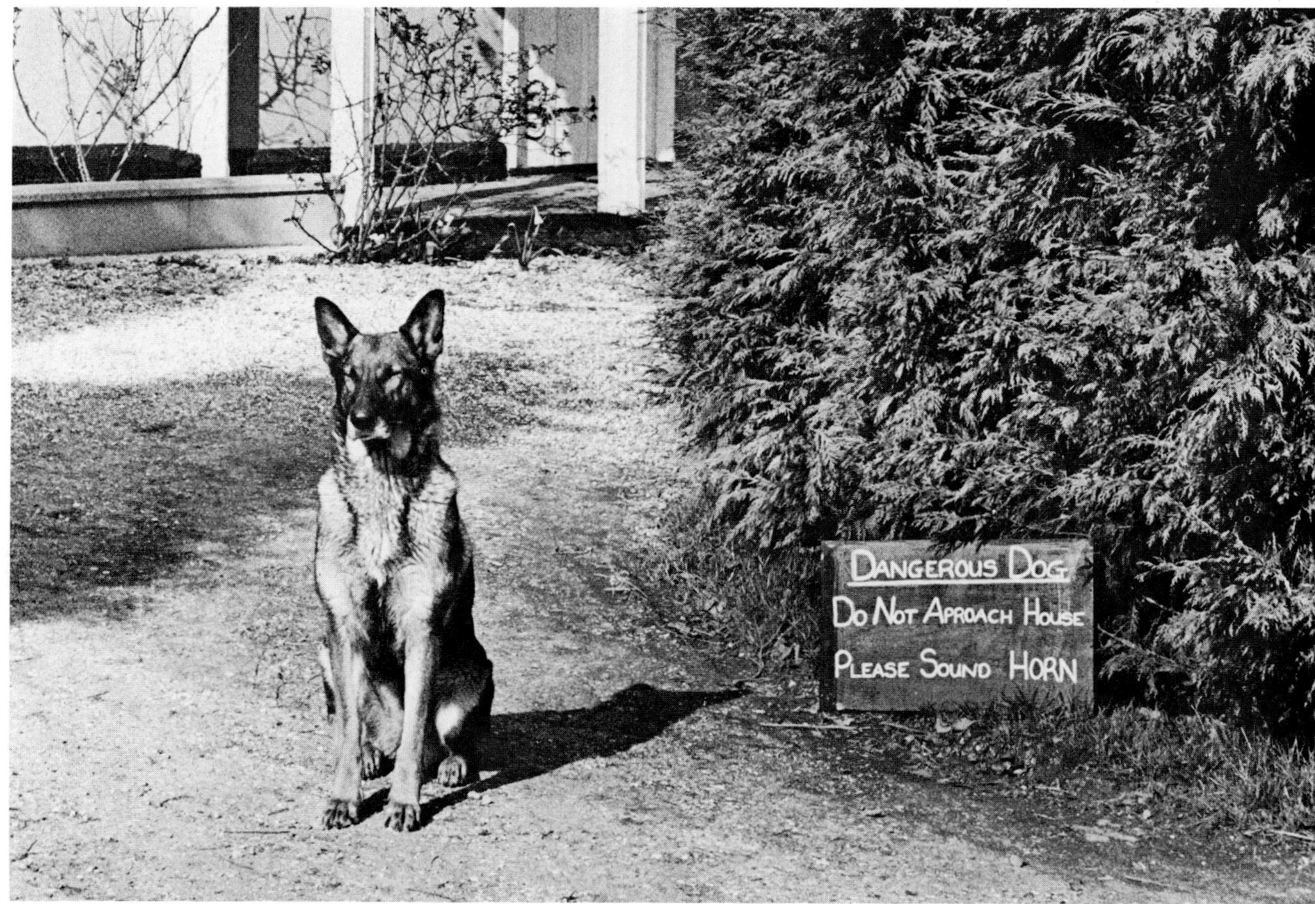
DANGEROUS DOG
DO NOT APROACH HOUSE
PLEASE SOUND HORN

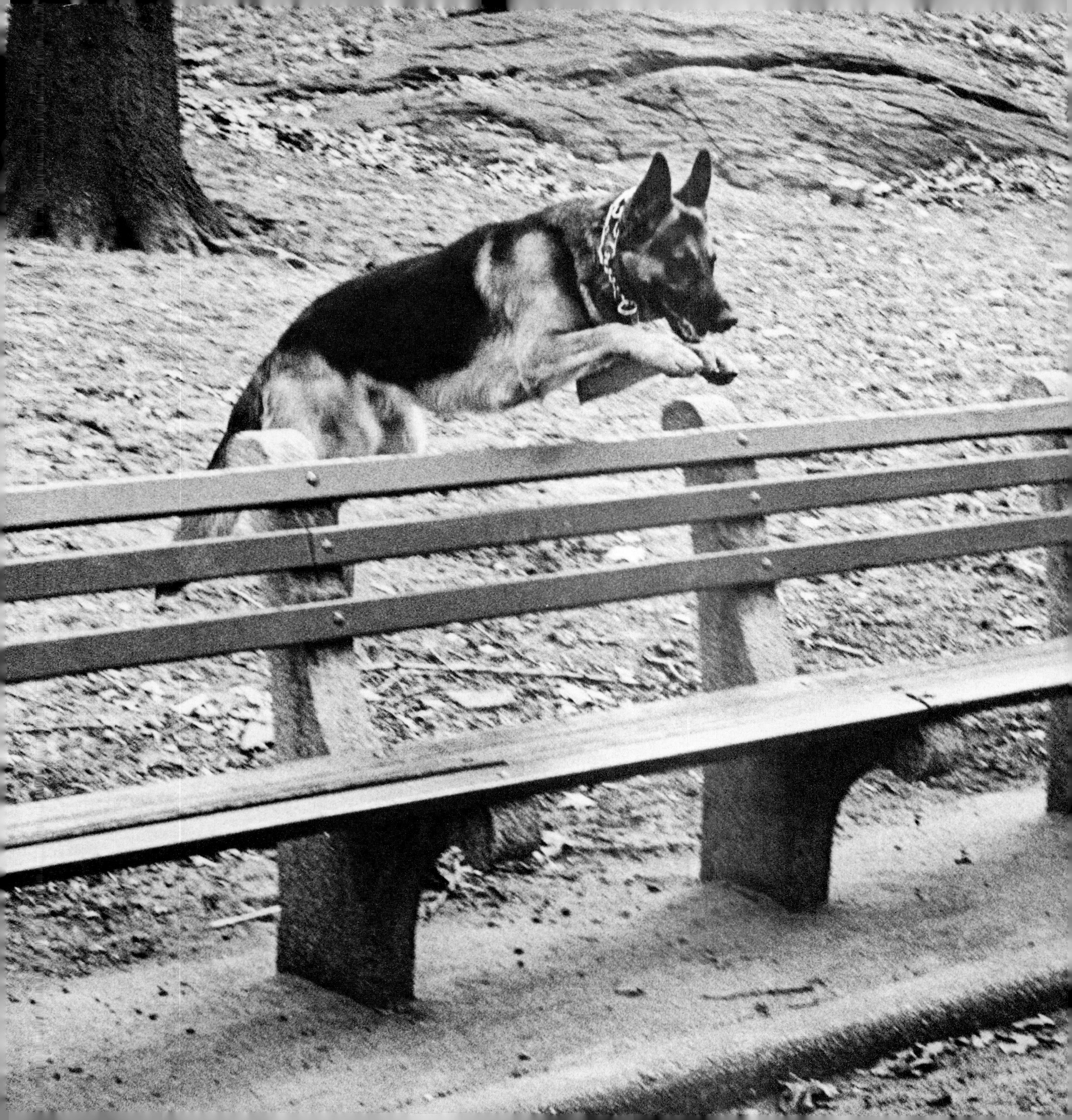

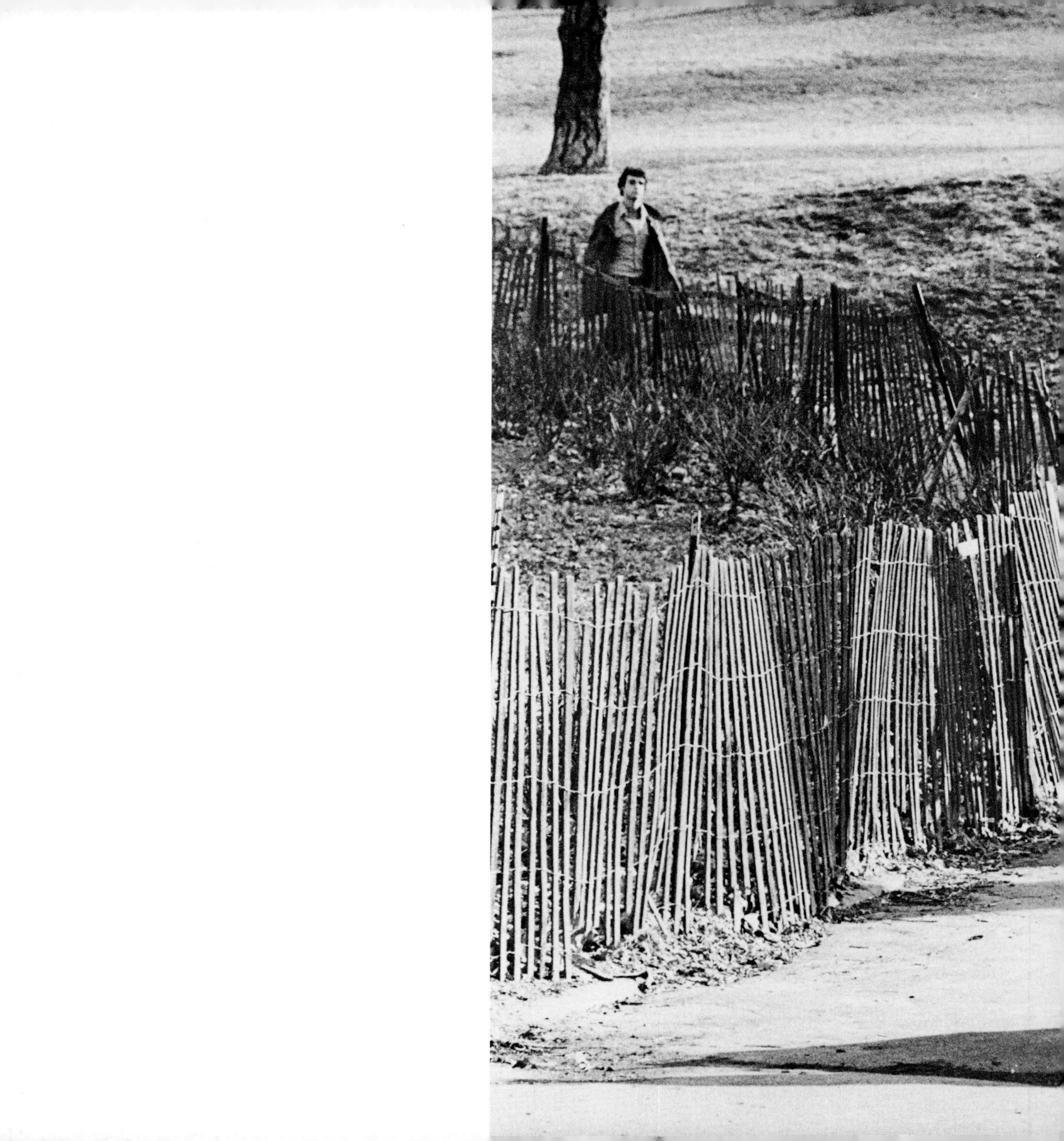

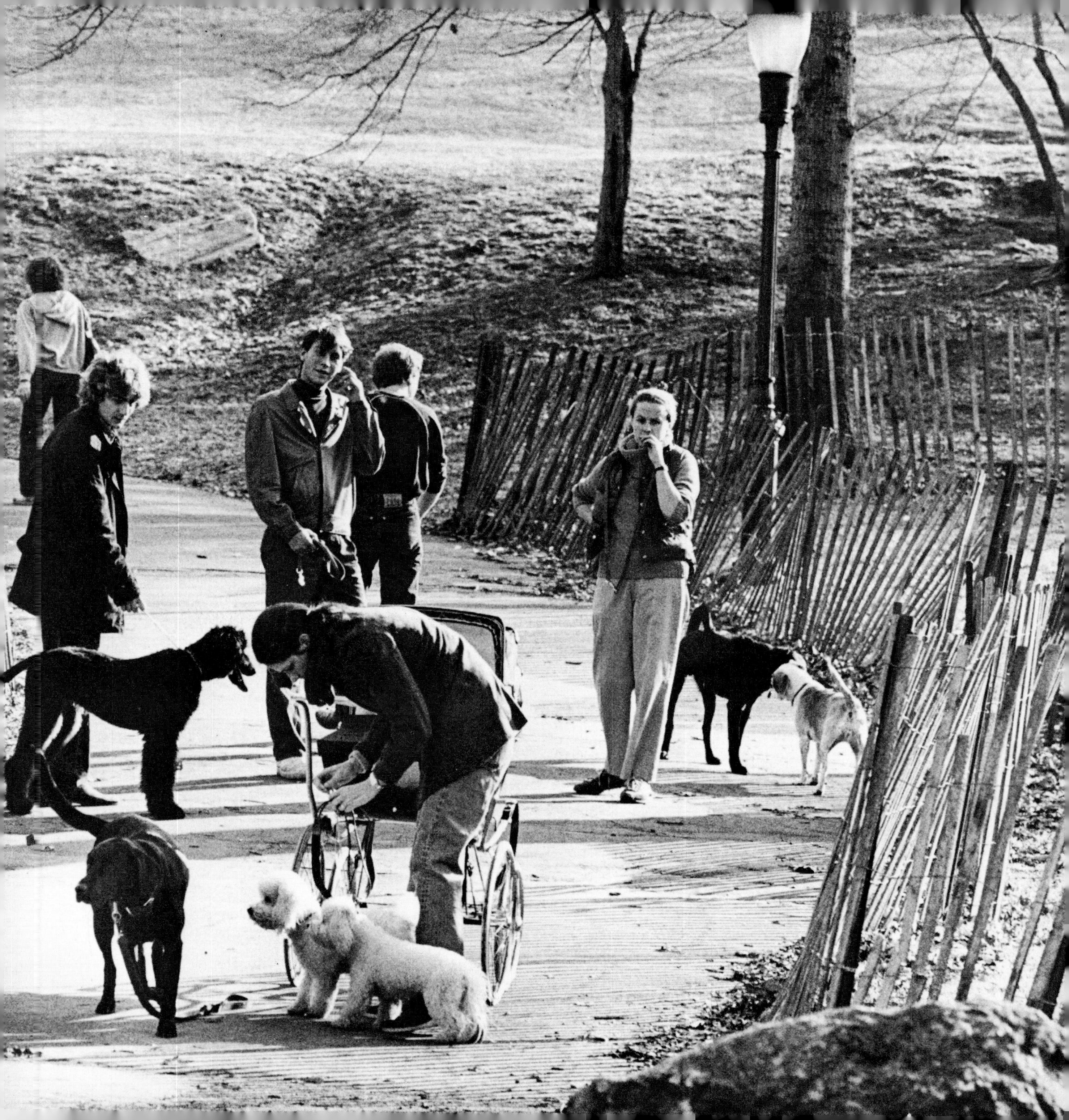

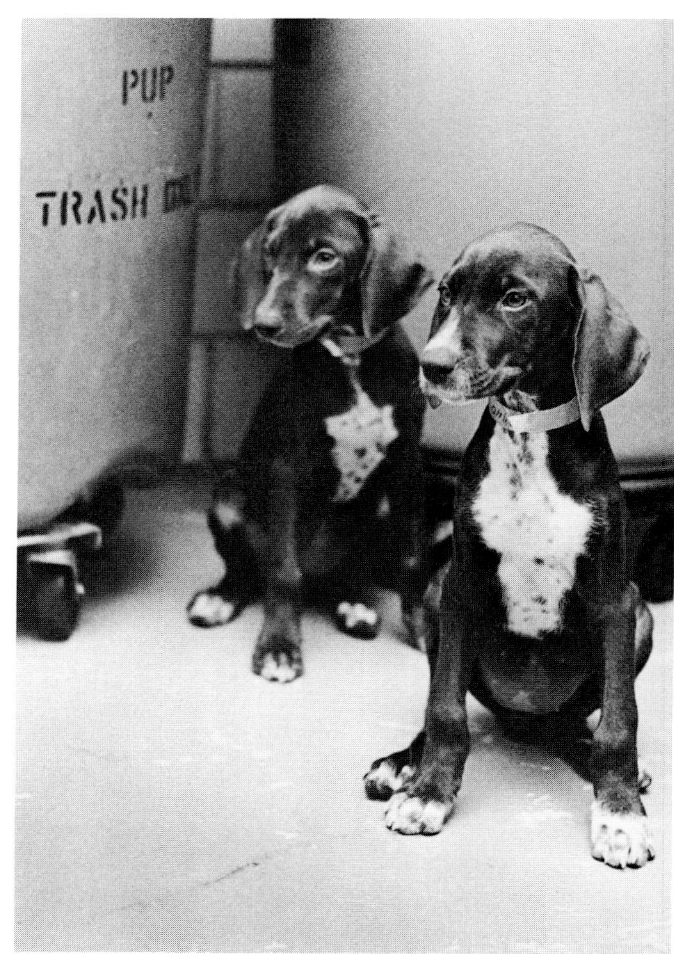
PUP
TRASH

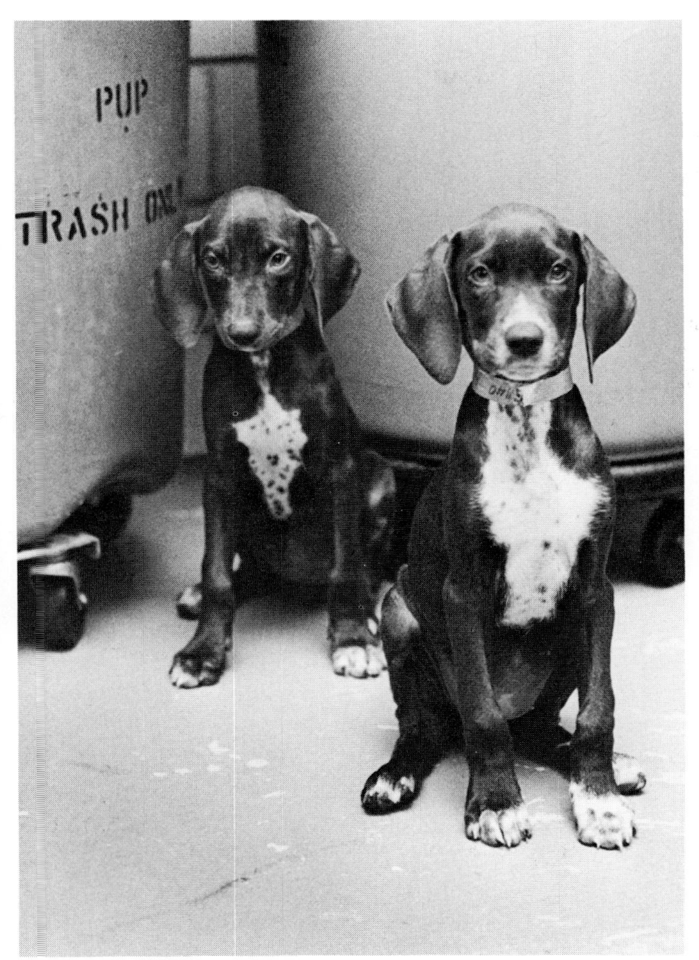
PUP
TRASH

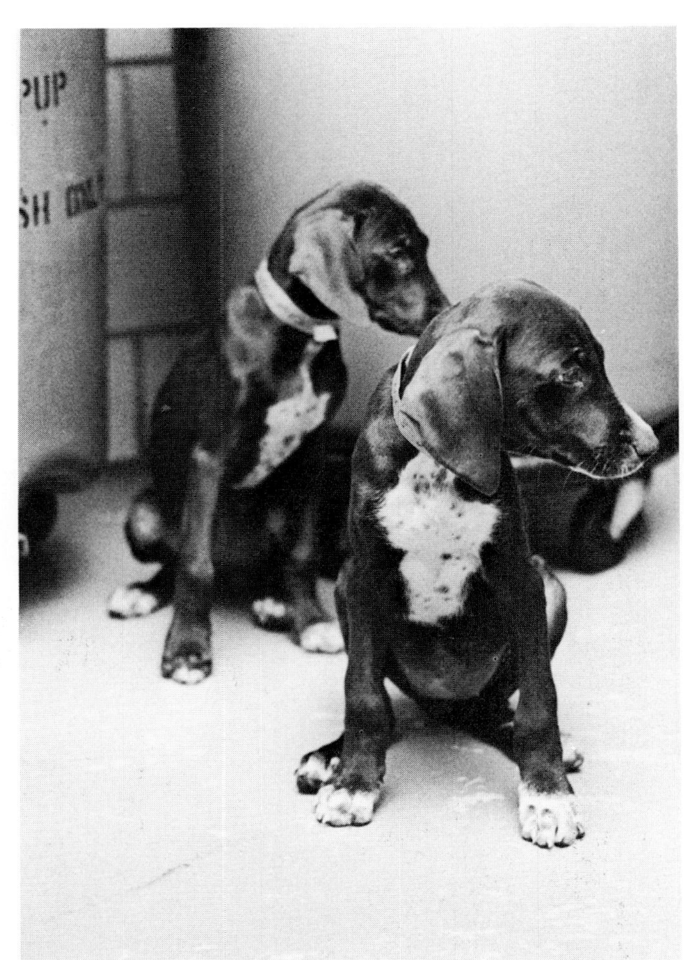
PUP

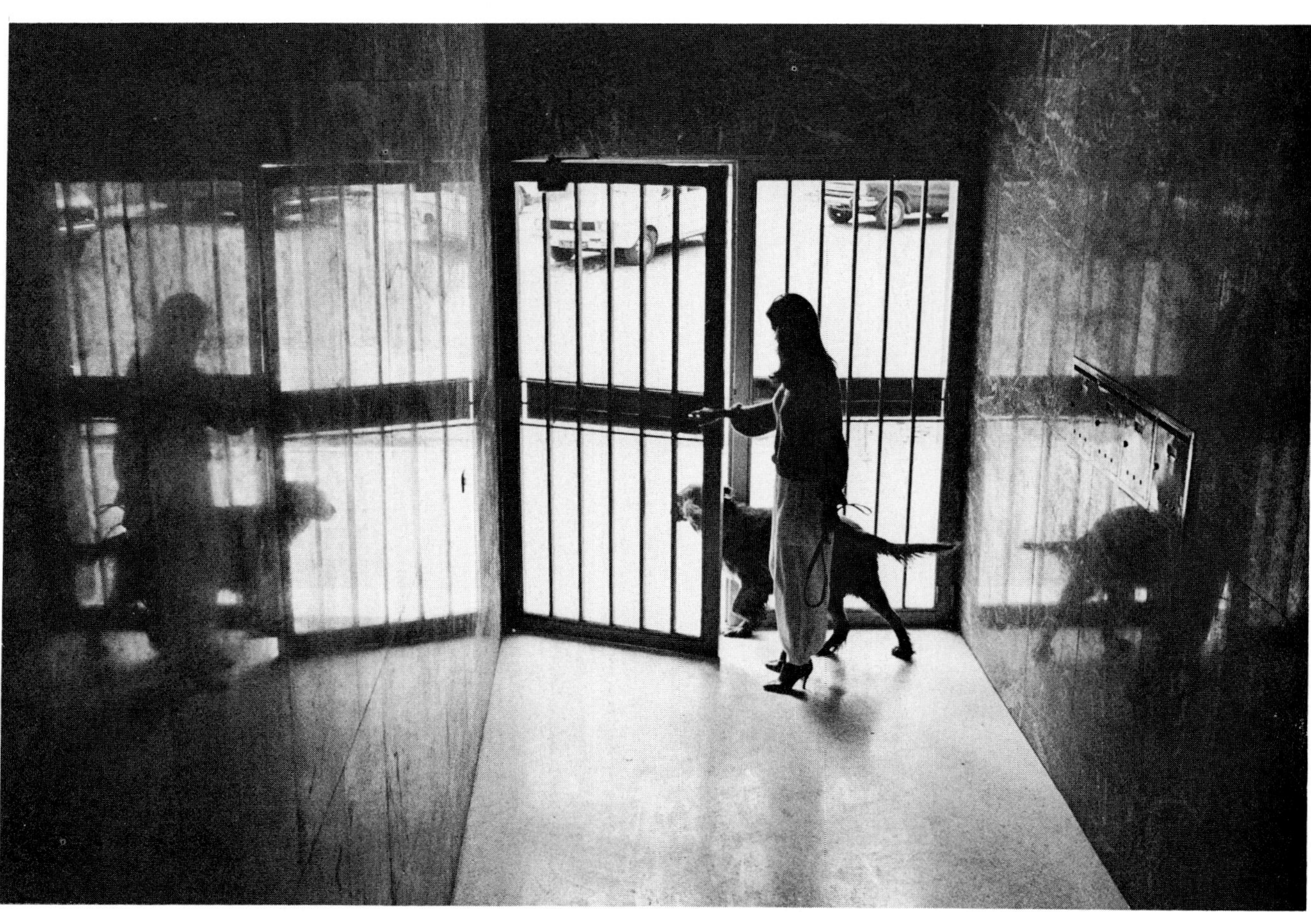

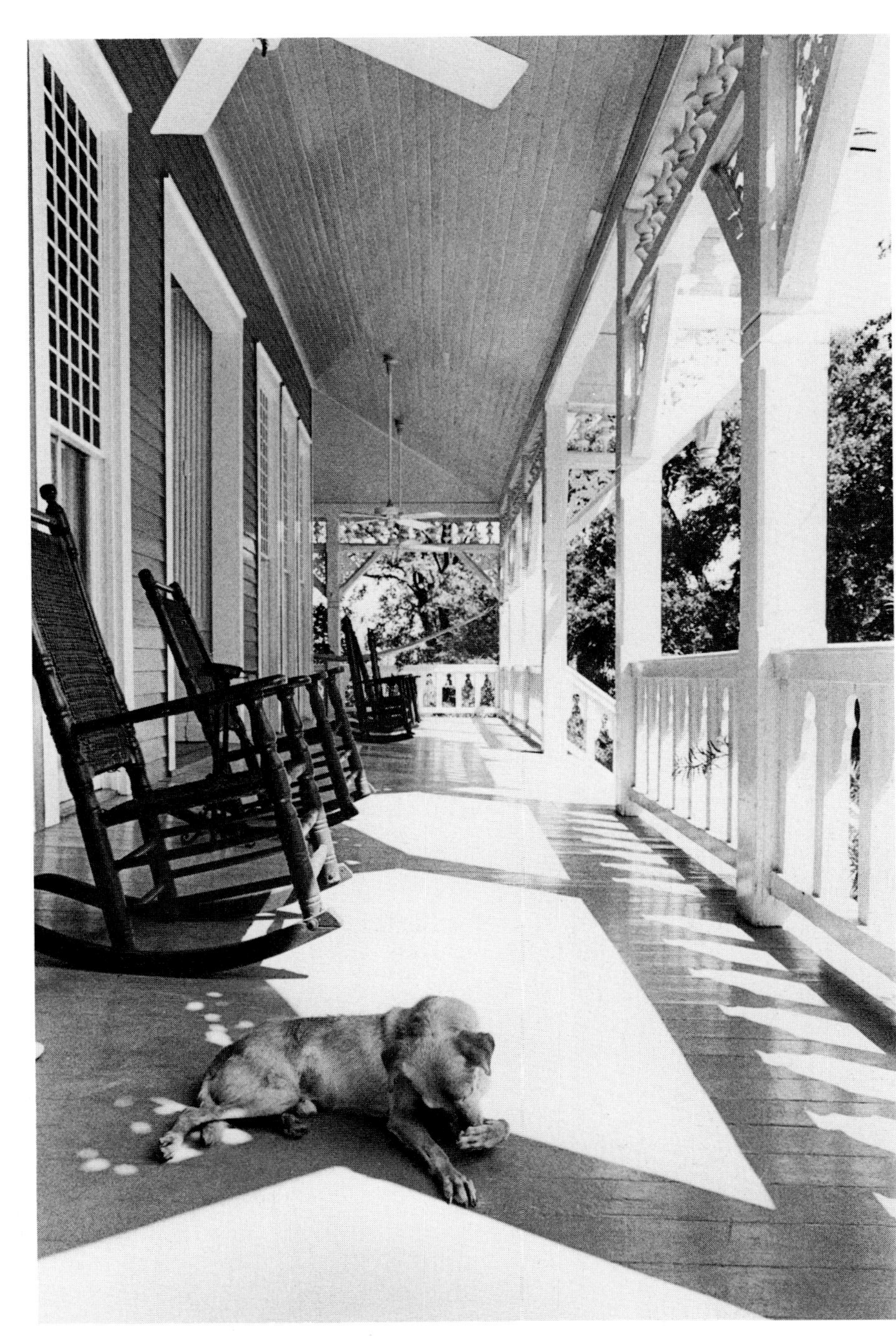

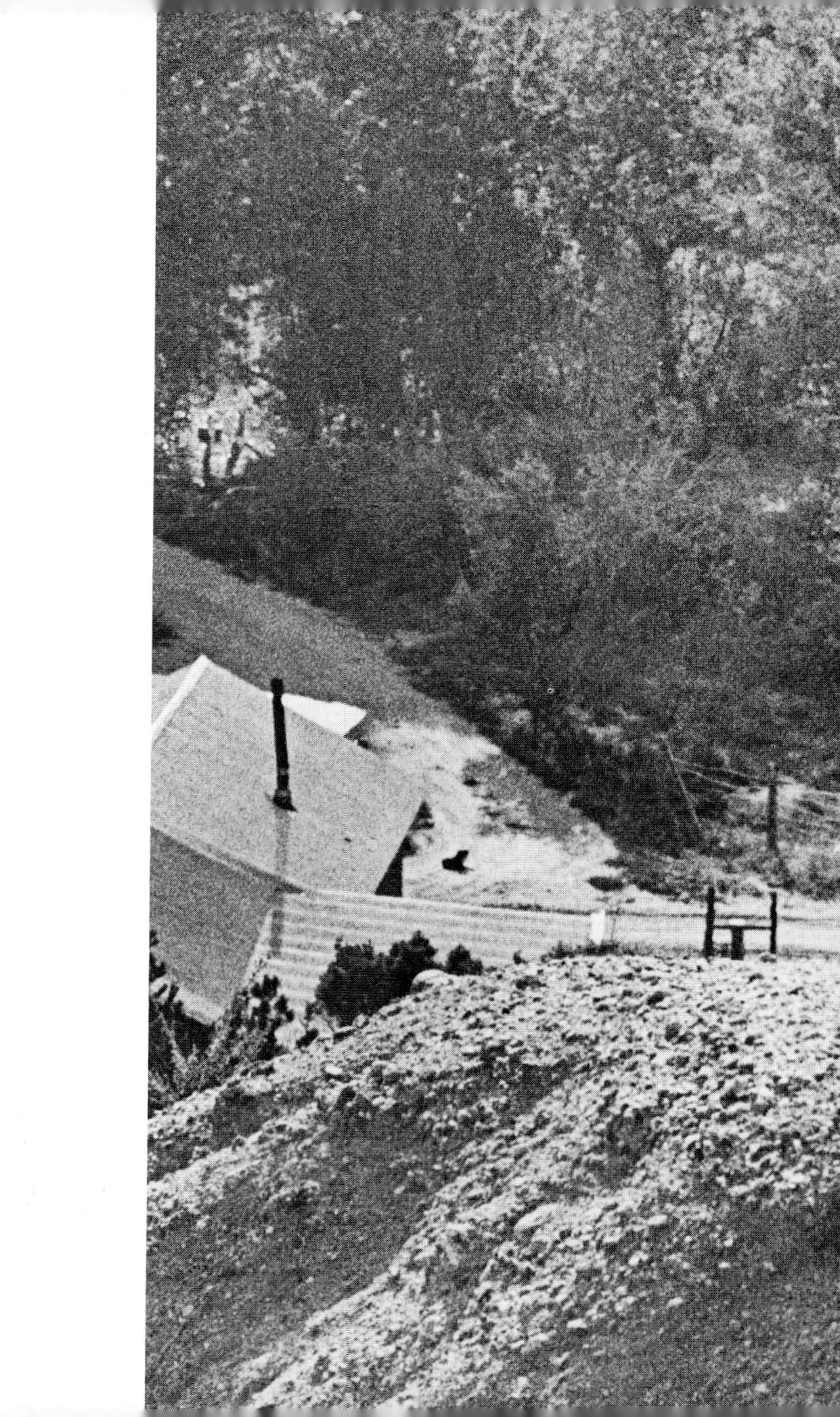

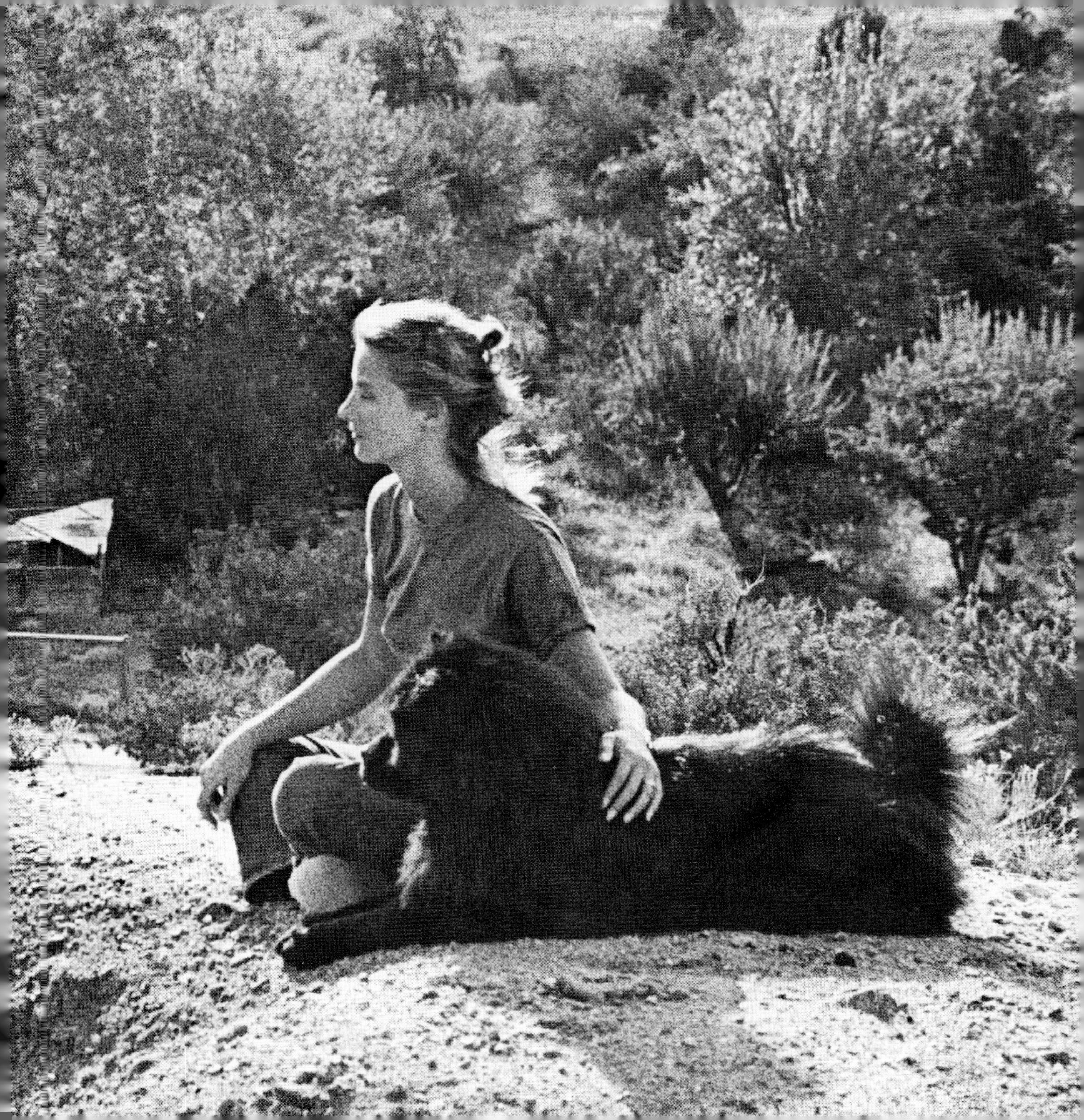

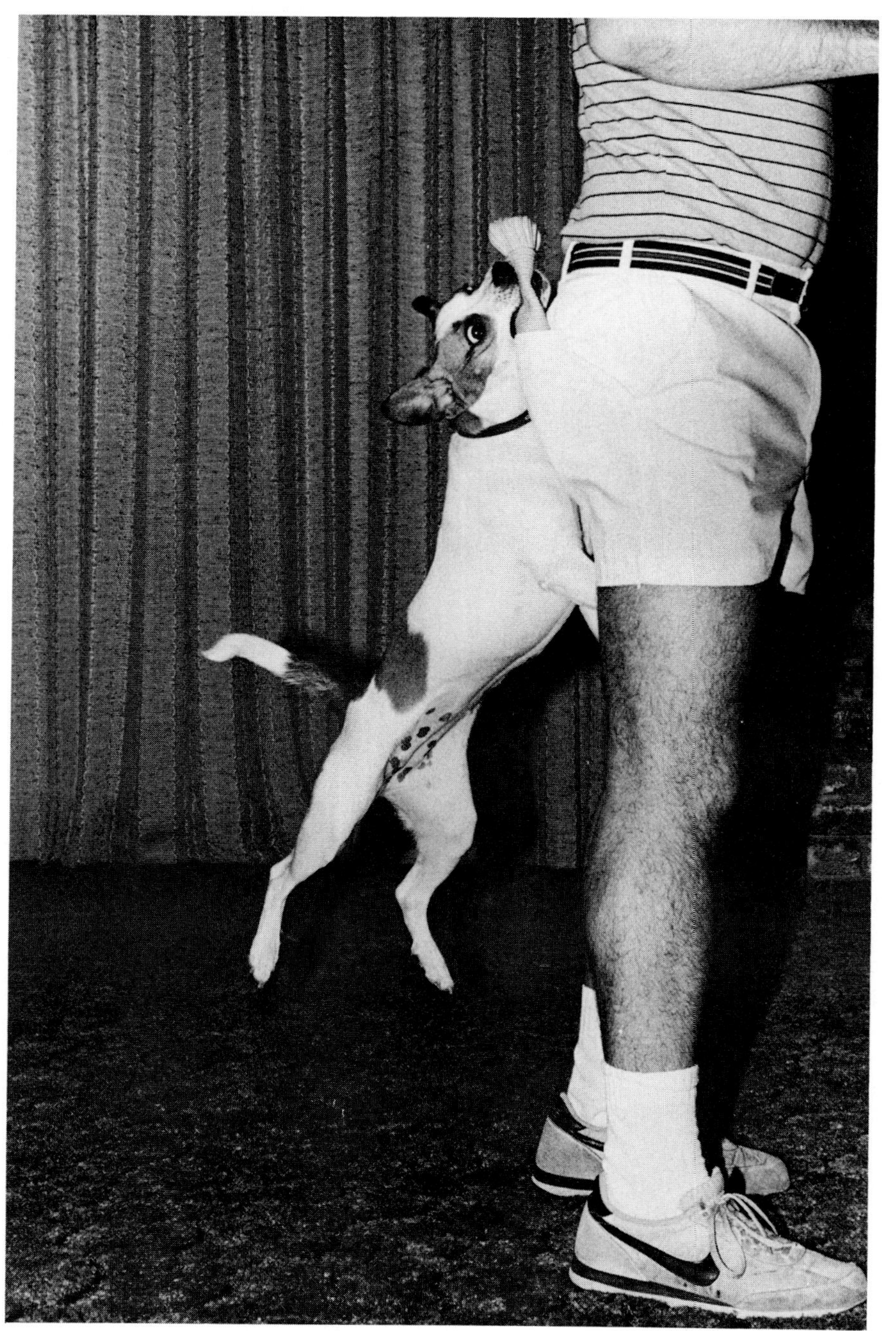

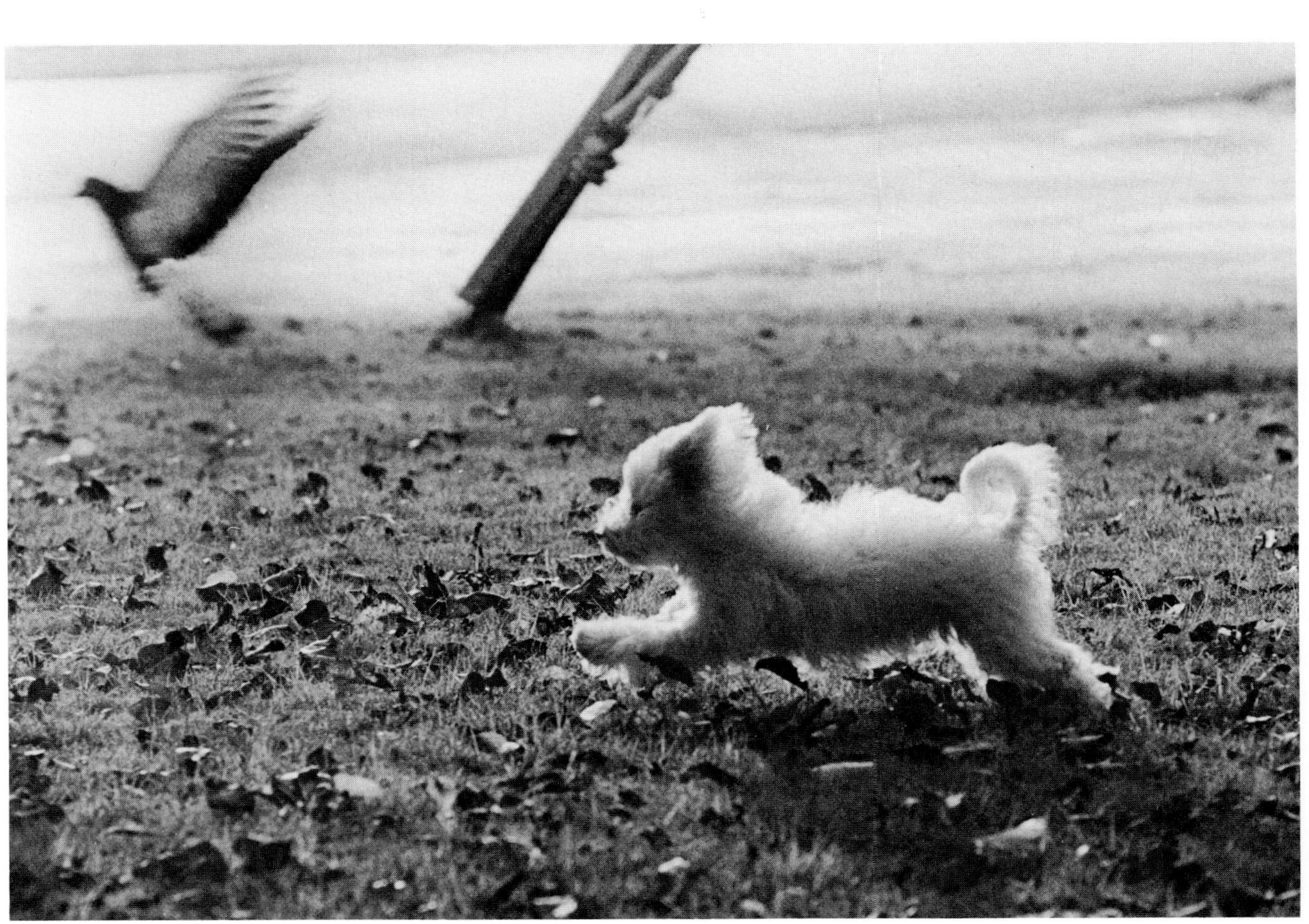

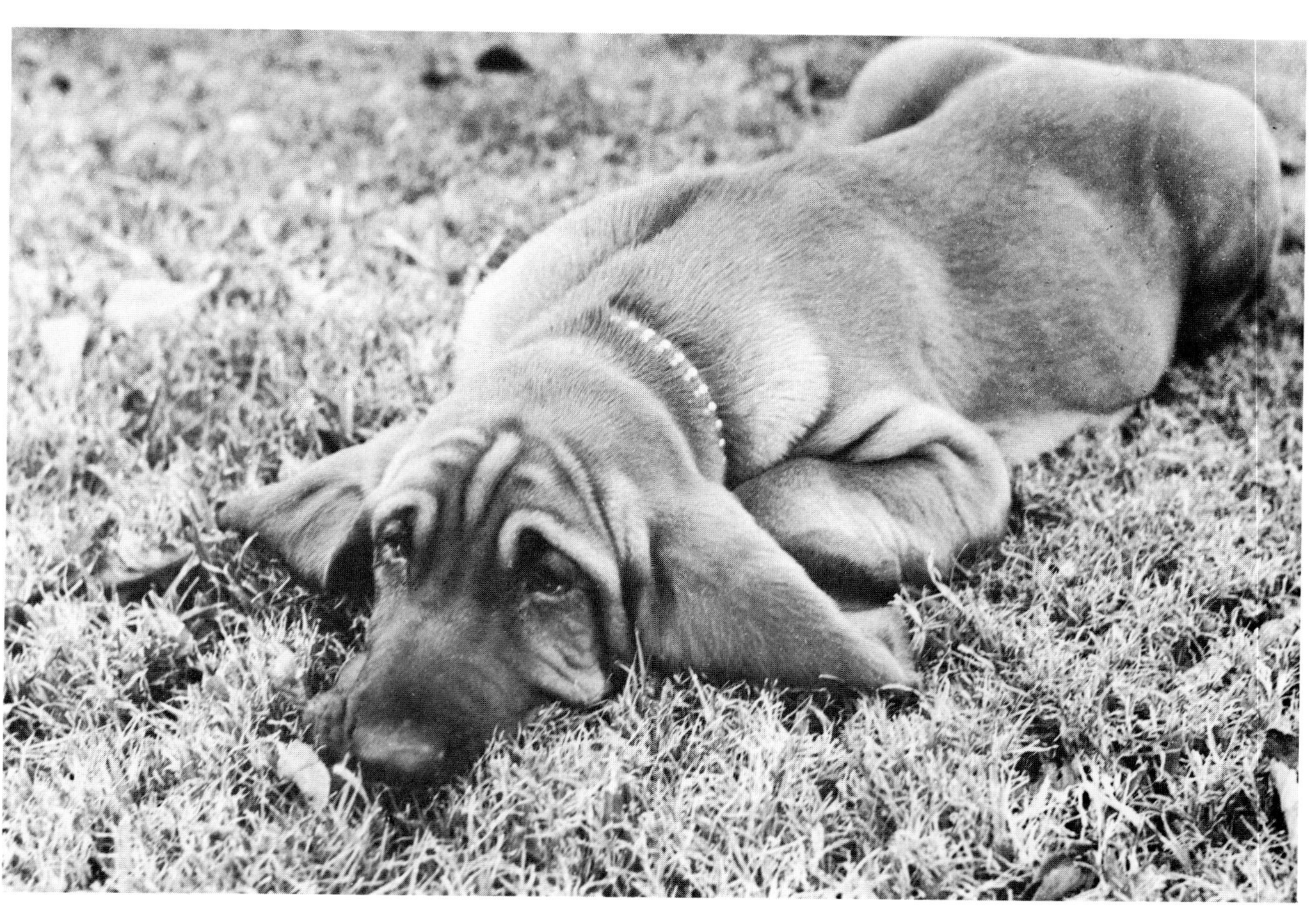

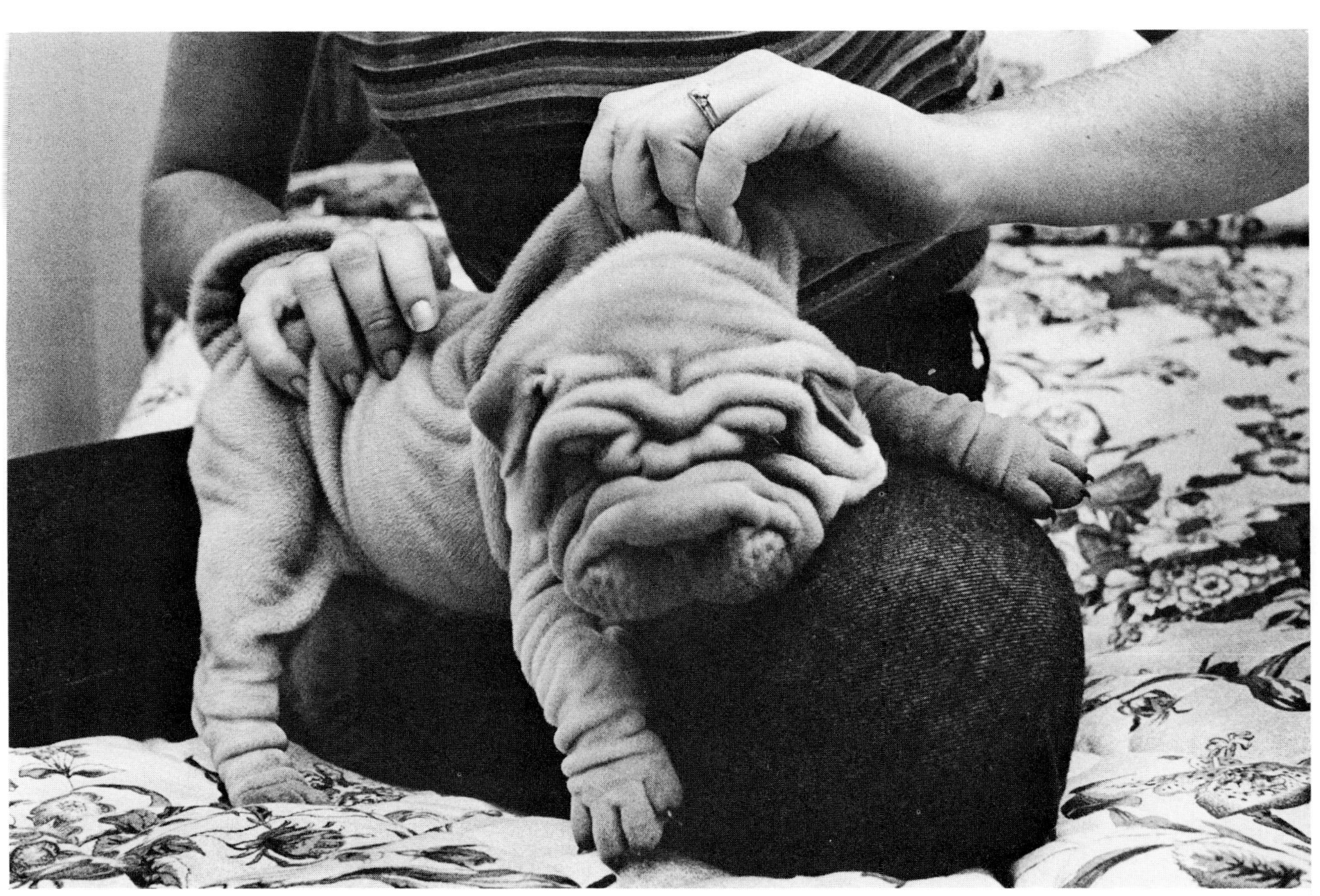

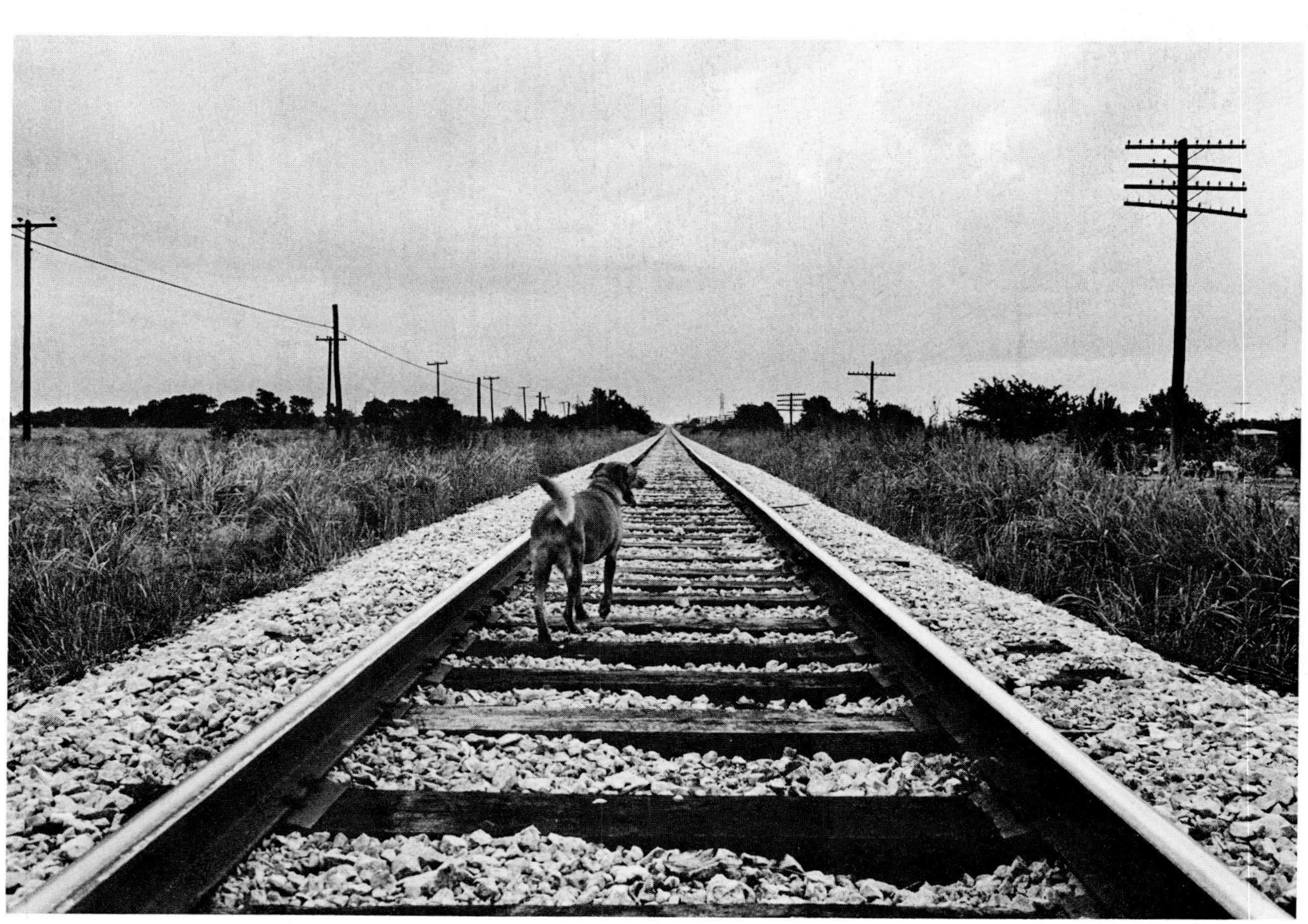